THERE'S A DANCE IN THE OLD DAME YET

Harriet Robey

G.K.HALL & CO.
Boston, Massachusetts
1982

Robey, Harriet.
There's a dance in the old dame yet.

Published in large print.
1. Robey, Harriet. 2. Widows—United States—Biography.
3. Aged—United States—Biography. 4. Large
type books. I. Title.
[HQ1058.5.U5R6 1982b] 305.2'6'0924 82-15739
ISBN 0-8161-3478-2 (lg. print)

An Atlantic Monthly Press Book

Published in Large Print by arrangement with Little, Brown and Company

Set in 18 pt English Times

To Alec
in fine, vivid, strong memory

MARGARITAE SORORI

A late lark twitters from the quiet skies;
And from the west,
Where the sun, his day's work ended,
Lingers as in content,
There falls on the old, gray city
An influence luminous and serene,
A shining peace.

The smoke ascends
In a rosy-and-golden haze. The spires
Shine and are changed. In the valley
Shadows rise. The lark sings on. The sun,
Closing his benediction,
Sinks, and the darkening air
Thrills with a sense of the triumphing
night—
Night with her train of stars
And her great gift of sleep.

So be my passing!
My task accomplish'd and the long day
done,
My wages taken, and in my heart
Some late lark singing,
Let me be gather'd to the quiet west.
The sundown splendid and serene,
Death.

by WILLIAM ERNEST HENLEY

CHAPTER 1

Alec was seventy-nine, I seventy-five on that December morning in 1975. I set out for work as usual. Alec had had intestinal flu over the weekend, but was able to eat some breakfast, so I left him, in his new blue paisley dressing gown, on our big double bed, little dog Snoopy beside him and the paper in his hand—obituaries to be read first, then the news. The heavy wet snow that had fallen in the night made our narrow road a tunnel in fairyland, aglitter in the sun. Great soft plops of white fell upon the car as I passed.

At eleven I telephone. He answers abruptly: "I've passed out twice this morning."

"Home in twenty minutes." I drive fast, enter the house, and look in the living room. There is a man on his knees, his arms up the chimney, and a sooty sheet on the hearth. I am puzzled; we had the flue swept very recently; what was Alec up to?

The man says, "Mr. Robey fell when he opened the door. I helped him to bed."

Quickly I move to our bedroom. He lies there, as usual when asleep, on his side, one hand under his cheek, one arm loose across his body, ankles slightly crossed. Snoopy lies beside him. I speak. There is no answer. I touch him. No response. I know a shrill alarm. I can't get his pulse. I can't see the rise and fall of his chest. I call his doctor and get him immediately. "He doesn't move," I say. I hear the doctor on another line calling the police. "Over in a few minutes," he says.

Now I stand there, and know and thank God, since dying has been so easy for Alec. I have always known he was afraid of sickness and death.

I'm still in a daze, looking at him, when four large men in fire clothes and heavy boots rush in. At once they are swarming over the big bed, pumping on Alec's chest, then giving oxygen, then doing resuscitation again. The fire chief arrives and one of the men shakes his head at him. The chief suggests I go to the other room. I do not want to. I want to see Alec come alive.

The doctor hurries in, the men get off the bed, and I go into the hall. In a moment he comes to me and says, "He's gone. Cardiac arrest." I go into the living room. The chimney sweep is still kneeling on his cloth on the hearth.

"Mr. Robey is dead. Please go."

"I'm just finished." He gathers everything up and he and the police cars leave. The doctor sits with me now. "Which undertaker do you want?"

"You know us. You decide."

He calls.

I am working on an emergency basis, thinking clearly, feeling nothing. I call one of our children, state the news and ask her to spread word to the others.

Now time telescopes. Undertaker arrives. He is nice and friendly and extremely un-undertakerish. I am reassured; I remember the horror of my mother-in-law's death, when Alec and I together in the great hushed and darkened rooms picked out a casket for cremation (do they use them again afterwards?—certainly they won't burn). And then we discussed details. The unctuous man said, "How did the modom fix her hair? (Yes, we have a special hairdresser who washes and sets.)" "But for cremation?" "Oh yes indeed. It's always done. And please bring some of her best clothes as soon as possible." By this time Alec was out of sight in another hushed room.

So here I sit opposite my undertaker.

"Have you got a wooden coffin? Can you get me one, a plain pine one?" He is incredulous. "My husband wanted a wooden coffin and I'll tell you why."

I find myself for the first time ever telling one of Alec's favorite stories—and I *am* Alec, with the Down East accent, the head-scratching, the belching, the spitting that the story demands. Briefly, it concerns two strangers who walk into the workshop of a Maine Yankee boatbuilder one night. They demand that he build them a coffin by morning, bribe him with a quart of whiskey, and leave. The boatbuilder creates his coffin while finishing off the quart. In the morning the strangers return, only to point out . . . The punch line, uttered in incredulity and delight, is "Jesus Christ! I put a centerboard in it!"

Am I quite mad? The undertaker has the grace to laugh heartily and says, "I'll get you that wooden coffin!"

The doorbell rings. I answer it. There stands a very timid, embarrassed-looking chimney sweep, who says, "That will be thirty-five dollars, please." And then, "I'm sorry." I grab my purse and give him the money. He is out the door just as our children begin to arrive. As my husband is taken out, one of our sons helping to carry, Snoopy jumps into the open back of the hearse and sits beside Alec. He has to be carried back into the house and the door closed. The whole situation begins to take on a Kafkaesque quality.

The rest of the day I am borne along like an inane bit of flotsam on a wave of people and activity. When bedtime comes I raise my voice. I want no one, but no one, in the house with me. Purely mindless, I am instinctively obeying the implicit rule of the family "Never give in. Never indulge yourself. Master!"—a rule that, since I was naturally timid, had resulted in making me more afraid of fear than anything else. I shove the last child out, lock the door, go robotlike through preparations for bed, and, although geared up for a night of pain, sleep solidly till dawn. Nature knows when to be kind.

Out of shock, out of the confusing river

of people, flowers, food, beginning letters all flowing in the front door; out of the eddy of calls, condolences, advice, decisions, even of my own automatic actions, my memories of that week are limited to four.

One: a minister, the minister, the first I have ever called upon or communed with in need, and now My minister, working out the service with me. There is strength in his quiet listening and he does not use the word *God* or try to comfort.

Another: I am in the little white eighteenth-century church with its high pews and plain altar. I study the right effect for the candlelit memorial service on Friday night when the grandchildren will have arrived from college. I find the florist able to follow my emotional fumblings. Nothing on the altar but one enormous spread of bright red carnations and those huge wiggly tortured white Japanese chrysanthemums. Dimly I wonder about a certain symbolism in my choice.

And another. At a moment when our three sons and our son-in-law are present (all are over six feet two, like Alec), I bid them, "Clean out his closet, everybody. Take all you or your kids can use. Everything else out and to the Good Will. Everything, except the soft knit undershirts. Those make good dusters." But I quickly snatch from my oldest son's hand Alec's blue Viyella dressing gown, my last gift to him, which the undertaker had removed from his body at my request, and I hang it in my closet as a shrine of sorts (later to touch, to feel, to put my cheek against, even to wear a few times with the sleeves turned up).

And on that Friday night I walk into the church on my oldest son's arm, and I force my head high and afterward I stand in the vestibule thanking people for coming and some I ask back to the house and when I finally reach home our narrow road and driveway are so solid with cars we can't get near the door. I have to walk. The place is aroar, and the young have done so well in the way of food, drink, and hospitality that the gathering of sad and sympathizing relatives and friends has turned into a fine party.

After the last guests are gone we sit until midnight around the fire. Grief, humor, and reminiscence: children and grandchildren are welded in joint sadness and finality, yet a kind of happiness, bonded even closer together than before. It is after midnight when the last of the young leave. I stand with my hand on the doorknob until the final sound of cars fades. And then, as if struck, I see everything brilliantly and horribly. I am now alone. Of Alec and our life together nothing is left but ashes. I am only half a person; the other half of me is in that urn. And I am—I shudder at the awful word—a *widow.* Forever! And so begins, in truth, my bereavement.

CHAPTER 2

Just a week after Alec's death I returned to my job as psychiatric social worker in a mental health clinic. What else was there to do! The first compassionate looks and sympathetic words of the staff were painful, but it was my nine-thirty group of eight mothers that was hardest to face. These women each had a "problem child." As we gathered and I looked at their wide watchful eyes and their tense bodies, I knew I did not need to tell them. And as we were a close group I thought, "They're caring and they're anxious." Nobody spoke till we had our coffee in hand, and then I told them that Mr. Robey had died just after the group ended last week, but died without apparent distress, and with moist eyes I spoke of my sadness and of how I knew they were sad for me, and why didn't we spend this session on grief, since even for the comparatively young there can be losses to the heart. It was an incredibly fruitful hour and a half. Not only in evoking past pain that I could see was related to the problems with the individual children, but in providing an extra springboard from which to work subsequently. Also I knew that the communal sharing had brought us even more trustingly together.

To a lot of my friends, social work is still slightly suspect, a case of the blind leading the blind. For others—friends who have quietly trod their own paths, limping or not, a social worker is almost as bad as a shrink. In 1945, when I became one, a social worker was still considered by many to be in the category of the washed-out spinster or the busybody do-gooder—sweet tenderness, baskets of food, cast-off clothing (but washed and clean), a mind full of sermons and uplifting reproaches at poverty and its causes. There were, of course, a few famous settlement-house workers, a few prison reformers, but one couldn't remember their names. And, in fact, I did refuse to become a fully dedicated professional, and later turned down two opportunities to teach, full time, in graduate schools of social work. A professorship would have added luster and prestige to my ego, but it would have involved a lot of off-duty responsibilities. More important to me were Alec and the simplicities of rich womanliness. I never worked full time and every so often I took a year off to become exclusively wife, housewife, mother, and grandmother. Yet I never reentered the arena of middle-age and older women whose husbands had not yet retired. I was lost to the round of volunteer work or committees, or entertainment such as sports, bridge, lunches, teas, or movies.

Why do something so different? A few years earlier, at the age of thirty-nine, I had scandalized my friends and much of my stiff-upper-lipped Yankee clan by going into psychoanalytic treatment, and had found it so helpful that—at last—I felt empowered to help others. The predicted expense of analysis was so great that I had had to approach my parents for a loan. My clan does not talk about feelings. But I said openly that I was very depressed from unknown causes, and had found that my own bootstraps of will were not strong enough to haul me up and out without insight. To my amazement, Mother at once cried out, "If it will save you from what I felt with my mother . . ." Words quickly shut off and never referred to in any way again. I doubt if she knew she had even said them. Father merely remarked in his quiet and rather quaint way, "Harriet's always been a sensible girl and if she feels this is right we'll back it." Wonderful parents! For Mother must have instinctively guessed that this step would insidiously separate me from her by breaking my emotional dependence on her, which, Alec claimed, was far too deep.

Once well into analysis my blood and brain were stirred to a life they had never known before. Afterward, with World War II upon us, two of our sons in the navy, Alec very busy and seemingly content, with the government quite typically but irrationally calling for some thousands of trained psychiatric and medical social workers at once (more than were registered in the entire country), with a tremendous drive within me to help others as I had been helped, I tried to enter a graduate school of social work, only to be turned down flat because of my advanced age, forty-three, because my college grades of over twenty years before had been so low, and because, chiefly, no one over thirty had ever been able to last out the hard training—so they said. Persistence over weeks got me one foot in the door. Then I moved fast, to prove to myself and the school that women like me, who had become mature through the experience of wife- and motherhood, who had learned to be sensible, wise, giving, and reasonably controlled, who possessed a strong desire to serve and were also willing to learn a whole new use of self, could run rings around the younger graduates in the profession.

After bereavement, work was my salvation. Work: dealing with clients in trouble and pain, whether as individuals, couples, families, or groups. Work, where there was order and habit and rhythm. Work, where staff, though very fond of their by-far oldest member, gave no quarter whatever. Work, where you had been trained to leave the problems of one client in clean safe escrow as you turned to the concerns of another one. Work, where angry feelings must be self-analyzed and where the expression of that anger must be rare, unimpassioned, realistic, and clean. Work, where creativity has to flow in every interview, where you give all you can and ask nothing back except a slow if often uneven growth—for though you may be a catalytic agent you cannot be another's will. Work, where by helping others find their strengths, you too gain strength and grow with each bit of growth of each patient. A lovely phrase: "The helping profession." One of woman's best, where all her gifts—intuition, empathy, compassion, ESP, intelligence, restraint, and reliability—are of the essence.

For me in that bad time work was a challenge, a demand, a haven and a refuge where I was, for a few hours, no longer in pawn to grief. With my home empty of a human object to love, I needed my clients almost as much as they needed me.

CHAPTER
3

There was work and there was home, home where the heart should be, home where my heart must now labor through the hard task of mourning. "Grief work": a stock expression in psychiatry, and a true one.

Early morning . . . there was the alarm clock, now my responsibility, the weather report, little dog Snoopy to be let out, coffee to start, clothes selected (pants suits), fruit and coffee and newspaper in bed, sandwich made, dishes cleaned (Alec had always enjoyed doing this after I had gone), bed now often left unmade, quick dressing and off, taking the shopping list and squeezing through the door to foil Snoopy's determination to go with me.

Our house, next to last on a narrow dirt dead-end road deep in woods, was very isolated. Alec drove a powerful old Jeep that sported a plow. He kept the road and driveway clear of snow and often hauled out those who were in trouble. The older he got the more the mightiness of that car satisfied a need in him. Together we had hand-shoveled the path, slowly, he with his emphysema, I with my bad back. But that road out was always scary when icy and was a constant undercurrent of anxiety that winter. For almost half the way the ground dropped sharply on each side, without barrier except an occasional small tree, and there were two little hills that seemed like mountains, to be mastered before reaching level land. Snow, if not too deep, was fine, but in these thick woods any thaw meant ice, lasting ice, and ice I can do without, and for the next three months I shimmied up the first rise, sometimes only after several runs, crawled down the other side in low gear until at a certain bodily-felt point I shifted, gunned, and slewed and skidded and shuddered up the next, often barely making it with a last violent screaming spasm of the wheels. No longer did I have Alec to haul me out. That drive became a pure test of determination. "Who needs this?" I thought wearily. Some friends near our age would not come in all winter and we had never invited anyone but the intrepid. Parcel, newspaper, and milk delivery periodically balked and even the oil company deposited each fall a barrel of gravel on the two rises.

And on the way home from work I picked up mail and groceries, and then Snoopy always went through his acrobatics of welcome. Physically I managed. Carry on as usual. Be self-contained and uncomplaining. Don't make waves, don't lean on your children, set them an example of strength, and always wear a cheerful face. My mother, in her quiet sweetness, had faded inexorably on the vine of her widowhood, to go out at eighty-five years in a last whisper of breath; her mother had been hand-mind busy and creative until her death at ninety-two; Alec's mother, age eighty-two, said firmly after her husband's death, "I will die in three years: all my money will be gone then," and she did and it was. Whatever their inner turmoil, these women never expressed it. I could do no less.

Those early weeks the end of daylight was bad. No one sitting there. No one to share silence with or with whom to exchange even idle words. I yearned for Alec's sometimes annoying "come back" when I daydreamed for a moment. I trembled when I drove to strange places or went into a new store. I couldn't imagine inviting anyone to the house. How to feed them? My social life from now on would be only with widows: fair game for the unscrupulous, people said. A few last visitors appeared with their condolences and I found myself unexpectedly angry, too raw to know what they might be feeling or what their awkwardness bespoke. How could they be spontaneous in the face of my rigid control? But one friend walked right in the front door, came to me as I rose, put her arms tightly around me and said nothing at all—just held me. For the first and only time I sobbed. In broody moments I began to sense a destructive power of the dead over me: mother—father—Alec.

Though I remained quite whole at work, each day as I drove home I became half a person again, with a nasty empty riven feeling. Alec hadn't been out of my mind for fifty-two years. We were one. Was he happy, hungry, tired, angry, in pain, troubled, bored? Had he guessed when I was silently angry? Was I pushing him too much, was I filling his needs? I was one great emptiness now.

I did my best to keep busy and efficient at

home. I arranged for plowing of the road, the snowblowing of the path (a neighbor's offer); I brought in firewood; I kept the radio on for noise, any noise; I turned our king-sized bed into its two original singles—easier to make and I wouldn't be reaching out in sleep for Alec's warmth. I made myself stop shutting the curtains at sundown and locking and relocking the front door. Daily I answered a half dozen of the loving letters. I had never dreamed I would welcome them so. I would never hesitate to write one again.

But the several Christmas parties people compassionately asked me to were as dry and alien as chaff in the mouth. Boring and inane. The checkbook wouldn't balance within hundreds of dollars. Every mechanical and electrical gadget obeyed Murphy's Law, even bottle caps. Sleep was but half sleep. Food was tasteless and it wasn't worth cooking for one. Alcohol no longer eased me but only threatened to loosen my control. Quite unrealistically I panicked over money. And I did one crazy thing. Without being aware, I bought, at the drugstore, a bright red lipstick. I stared at it when I got home. I don't wear lipstick!

Then depression and numbness laid its

great weight upon me and I could hardly move. But out of somewhere in my memory, from perhaps thirty years before, a poem by Georgie Starbuck Galbraith struggled to reform itself in words, and after a few tries I got it.

What do I do till the life comes back
To the nerveless flesh and the stoic brain,
Till the blood can rouse itself to speak
To the icy blood in the frozen vein?
In time the blessed tears will start
As senses quicken to the rack
Of vital pain, but Oh, dear God,
What do I do till the life comes back?

I was very silent with that one for a few days, feeling it fully; and then life with its rack of pain did come back, but in irrational jerks, and with a sense of loss that had neither meaning nor reason to it, a sort of madness, and my mind wanted to crawl into a hole and bury itself ten feet deep away from pain forever. Gretchen! I remembered little dog Gretchen. Years ago we had had English fox terriers for our children. Gretchen and Mickey they were named, from the same litter, trotting out their lives together as they investigated the countryside, Gretchen always a few paces behind her mate. They adored the children.

One June night Gretchen turned up without Mickey and soon we found he had been killed by a car. The two younger children, the only ones at home, were to leave for camp the next day; their grief made them reluctant to go, but they must. On my way back from the station where I saw them off, Gretchen constantly jumped from back to front to back of the car. When we reached the house she started to dig a hole next to the nearby stone wall. The dirt flew. Her behavior was so curious that I stood and watched, aware of a strange inner anxiety. For after each bout of digging she curled up in the hole—which was as yet no hole but only a shallow depression—then sprang out, dug again, curled up with nose down in the dirt, then out to dig frantically again, her little body so tense and her motions so rapid it was painful to watch. Whatever her intent, she could see or hear nothing—not my call or whistle, not the tentative honk of the car horn. The hole deepened, but not enough. There *was* no rest for her, I suddenly knew, and with tears in my eyes I picked her up bodily, carried her into the house and held her forcibly in my lap, her body jerking; her trembling, her deep trembling, was uncontrollable. I spoke to her as to a terrified child and stroked her, and so it went for most of the day. I knew now that the double loss of her mate and the children was too much for such a high-strung dog. That night I kept her, still shaking, under the covers with me; the next night, on the bed with my hand on her; and the third night on a soft chair where I could touch her. And gradually the trembling ceased. But she followed me like a shadow until the children returned. Then she was playful once more.

It was a help to know, then, that there is added to our realistic and immediate sense of loss a deep atavistic pain and bewilderment that can lead to a kind of madness: a profound instinctive recoil at the unknown and forever unknowable that blinds and terrifies. (Why else do we dress up our corpses as if they were going to a party?)

That craziness passed, though not as quickly as had Gretchen's. Alec came alive again, bringing another kind of anguish —raising emotions as irrational as the red lipstick or a very sick heart. . . .

You, my love, are forever safe, forever free of bondage, pain, and sadness. Why can't you let me be at peace, too?

And you've left me with all your own pain and mine, your work and mine. You took away half of me; give it back!

You couldn't have loved me or you'd never have deserted me; it was a lousy marriage anyhow with your trying personality.

Why didn't you teach me financial details, taxes, tools, how to change fuses. Why didn't you make me do the checkbook?

—I'm nobody, nothing. No one comes or calls any longer. It was you who drew people to this house, not me.

—I'm too little and weak to do this alone, I'm a lone, lorn Mrs. Gummidge.

—I need you so, I loved you so. We were so happy together.

—I can't remember your ever doing or being anything but perfect. Your strength, your fine tall body, your tough tenderness, your humor.

—If I hadn't gone to work that day, or if I had phoned earlier, I might have saved you.

—Look what I sacrificed for you, what I put up with, how caged I felt while filling all your needs. You shackled my spirit.

—I could kill God who killed you, my man.

—I hated your limitations, your fussiness, your rudeness, the times you punished the children.

—Did I do enough? Was I too selfish and self-centered? I could have been more thoughtful. Did I castrate you in pushing through my own needs?

—Ours the perfect marriage, you the perfect lover, who gave unstinting love.

—If only I had known then what your and my mother went through, I might have helped them.

—I see you constantly, your fine face, beautiful hands, and muscular body. If you had been mutilated in an accident or an autopsy had been done, I couldn't have stood it.

—Your love for me and your patience were endless. I'm bitterly angry at you.

The various stages lasted anywhere from an hour to a few days, but so much poisonous food I could not digest.

Then one March night as I sat in my usual chair at dusk and looked at Alec's empty one, I became rigid in a culminating passion of grief, anger, self-pity, confusion, and emptiness. It seemed as if I could no longer contain myself within my body. Jump up! Scream! Do something awful and crazy!

That winter there had been a lot in the papers about the Transcendental Meditation movement, and I had found it vaguely interesting. And that very morning I had read an article by a respected physician who said that the body relaxation and the breathing were fine therapy but that the insistence on a special mantra was ridiculous. Any word, such as *one,* would do. Let each muscle relax in turn, breathe deep in the diaphragm letting the abdomen rise on the inbreath and contract on the outbreath, and say "one" at the exhalation. Out of my despair came a sudden impulse to try it. Step by step I relaxed as best I could. My breath went out, my abdomen contracted down. "One," I said. But I didn't say "one." I uttered the word *growth*. It shocked me. I tried again, and again came the word *growth,* beautifully extended out: "gr-o-o-wth." Was I out of my mind? I began to laugh at my gremlins. Was this a message from somewhere?

Well then, all right. Growth it would be, not helplessness and despair and the injured sense of "being done to" by fate. The thrust to be calm, to live fully again, began.

A tender little wind of change blew in my face. It was a timid wind at first and brought some guilt and shame, but it grew stronger into a funny kind of hope. I could say firmly to myself that I no longer needed to play a wife-mother-cook-nurse role. With no one to do for, what would it be like to be free? Free! In fright I drew back again, but my healing had begun. Grief was softer, my mind functioned better. I even did most of the income tax myself and was proud. I could stretch out to others and no longer expect pity from them, pity that I would hate when it came. Sometimes I could even reach and touch a peaceful empty place in myself.

I could see now that our marriage, any marriage, was like being a pair of lovebirds in a cage; and that we were happy there, more or less, although in the early days we thirsted separately to get out and fly wide and wild and free and alone. But we learned our space and came to sing within it. And then suddenly there was no more cage at all. The bars had dissolved at the very moment when one bird lay dead on the gravel of the floor. Must the other lovebird sit songless on its perch? Must it pretend the bars were still there, be afraid to feel freedom, afraid to fly alone? No, I would fly, and perhaps in time see our life together as a whole.

CHAPTER 4

Where were our/my children in all this? As I look back, they seemed to exist in only four incidents. I was too locked into myself to remember much except the fatigue of the effort to hide my malaise from them. (What a waste!) Had they not been loving and thoughtful throughout I would recall sadness or even bitterness, for I was too sore to tolerate slight.

It was in late December that a daughter-in-law urged me not to try to get to the office in snowstorms. "Be kind to yourself," she said.

In January my trustee son chided me for an impulsive and large donation I had made the end of December. I burst into ridiculous tears of guilt and shame.

In April another son flew in from the west to buy and install a Citizens Band radio in my car in case I should be in need on the road. I learned that *handle,* in CB jargon, is a self-given title. In my innocence I chose "Antique Beaver"—for in the booklet on CB words *beaver* meant *woman.* But when, at a road block or accident or on seeing a *"smokey"* (police trooper) on the road, I broadcast my handle (for I always stayed on the truckers' channel 19), I got a distinct impression of high glee from the thick vibrating voice that responded. It was later that I discovered that *beaver* had a distinctly sexual connotation. Well, then, let it be. It added to my enjoyment of life, and it hurt no one.

The fourth memory was with our second son, a doctor. Spring was here and all ice was out of the river. The scions of Thoreau's peepers in their annual demand for life space still shrilled from Fairhaven Bay where it stretched out below the house, and the first warm Sunday had arrived, the right day to scatter the ashes that had been waiting in their fine antique brass and copper urn on Alec's workbench—that center of all his retirement interests. My son and I paddled the canoe up to where the Sudbury River enters the bay, that some ashes might sink, some perhaps be carried by the current toward the sea. I took the cover off the urn and shook out the contents. Wonderingly my son remarked that he hadn't realized there would be so many bits of bone. Then we sat quiet, drifting, silent under the impact of the corporeal and the incorporeal. I cried a little.

But Alec's sometimes ridiculous humor visited even that ritual scattering. From the shore there suddenly came the scream of our burglar alarm (which simultaneously notified the police). Grief was broken through. We paddled hard and fast back toward the landing. On the steep rise above stood my son's wife, waving her arms and laughing with embarrassment. I ran up the hill as I alone knew how to turn the damned thing off. It was still screaming into the woods and the neighborhood.

She had been reading and waiting for us, and, noticing a small bell near her, had pressed it out of curiosity. It was the panic button. She had to go outdoors to escape the noise, but she canceled the police first. Together we could only laugh. The scene would have amused my sardonic Alec greatly. But I never had the alarm operative from that day on. I was more afraid of the noise than of any burglar.

CHAPTER 5

Now the heavy spring rains that thunder upon the earth had passed, as well as the intense contrasts of white clouds swiftly blown across brilliant blue sky that leave below sharp lights, stark shadows, heat and chill. All our birds had returned. And the quiet of late May and early June brought a wondering calm in which I needed to touch earth very simply—to go back to a time when the voice of the turtle was first known to me. And as I listened and waited I knew again, clear as a cowbell in mountain meadow, the gentleness of my childhood.

Sounds: crow of rooster, caw of crow, *huuu* of dove, bleat of lamb, drone of bees on rotting pears and velvet-blue grapes, hay-tedder click, clip-clop of horse on gravel, chug of rare slow automobile, insistent *whill* of whippoorwill, faint bark of dog, bay of fox, hoot of owl, the last unimpassioned *tee-whee* of a very sleepy robin.

Smells and tastes: spring-spread manure, sweet breath of cow, fresh baked bread with yellow butter and brown molasses on the heel, first tiny white violets, new-mown hay, apple-wood fire; lick of sea salt from forearm, squirt of warm milk from cow udder to open mouth, strawberry ice cream licked from dasher, pale lilacs by old cellar hole.

Sights: sky-blue bluebird, robin's jerk at worm, wrinkle of heavy cream on milk pan, bluebottle fly in web struggle, motes of dust sunlight-dancing, spit bubble on hot iron, silvery skin-shed of great black snake, flipflop to ground from under cow tail, beady eye of mean sow, slops and swill flowing from pail to trough, crawling mass of gypsy caterpillars, castles of white clouds in azure sky. And sometimes the hint of infinity.

Touch: warm new-laid egg, waxy black ice weaving under double runner skates, kidskin inside of chestnut burr, slippery frog-jelly cradled in palm, Flexible Flyer hurtling down too fast, spring-tender bare feet on gravel, high sway of swing and up-down of seesaw, thumb running down pea pods, somersaults on lawn, prickle of hay in mow; grasp of top branch of tall tree hard-climbed, touching the sky, learning our glorious perpendicularity to the earth.

These were the sounds of longing, the smell of life, the sight of birth or death, the touch of pain and emptiness, the feel of discovery, and the taste of shame. And always one or another of us four said, "Hey! I've got an idea!" And off we went exploring or creating or simply being, alone or together.

Few events punctuated the passing seasons. The circus in spring, going to the beach for the summer, Fourth of July, Halloween, Thanksgiving turkey and Christmas: a snowstorm deep enough to keep us from school, and visits to the dentist. And we played the inventive play, we four, of children almost without toys. But a great barn, an apple orchard, white birches to swing on, brooks to dam, hills to coast, potatoes and apples to roast over our little outdoor fire, hen-house tag on the various roofs—almost adjoining but of differing heights—helping care for the barn stock (but never allowed to learn to cook. Why?).

The adults in our lives? Teachers at

school. The grandparents (Grandfather handed out ten cents each time). Occasional visits from relatives, the hired man overseeing the barn and the land, the day of the ice wagon (we wiped sawdust off discarded bits of ice and sucked them), the milkman with his bottles clanking against the metal holder, the meat cart with the flies and slavering troop of dogs following and the roast carried in on brown waxed paper in an enormous hand, and the fish man whose cart stank. And there were the ubiquitous roving tramps who scared us a bit, and once a group of gypsies in wagons passing by, several women picking the lice out of their children's hair as they rode. And, of course, that rare automobile that we ran out to see.

Adults seemed absolutely reliable and fair, but stood for no nonsense whatever. Certain commandments had come down through a powerful matriarchy. They ran roughly as follows:

> Thou shalt not deliberately hurt anyone, including any living thing (some insects exempted; they breed disease).
> Thou shalt never tell a lie, or steal, or cheat.

Thou shalt be mannerly. Never shalt thou fail in courtesy to a social inferior.
Thou shalt never sit idle.
Thou shalt be unafraid at all times.
Thou shalt be pure in body, mind, and spirit.
Thou shalt never hate. Ever.
Thou shalt not know anger, nor exhibit any extreme emotion.
And thou shalt always do thy duty, no matter how unpleasant or difficult the task may be.

We learned love for our parents, and the ethos and mores of our tribe, and from school we brought back interesting new words. Reproof was given in a firm, strong unimpassioned voice that brooked no retort. Punishment? I don't remember any—only, very very rarely, the appalling sight of my mother's face distorted with uncontainable, silent revulsion at some unmentionable sin.

The poor children of today! They live in a cacophony and a kaleidoscope of sense impressions and stimuli so swift they would fuse into a blur, were it not for the human capacity to block out the excess. Constant TV, radio, police sirens, fire engines, whistles, trains, cars, enormous speeding trucks, flashing neon lights, vacuums and blenders and mixers and washers, bright plastic toys—more and more toys—and sweet foods, sweet drinks, snap, crackle, pop, and warnings of danger everywhere. "There's nothing to do!" comes the whine. More toys, more snacks . . . No time for a rock in a lap, no time for storytelling, no time for the stillness that leads to invention and discovery. Stillness is frightening, alone is frightening. Poor little things!

I rested within recaptured simplicity and planted my annuals, a little late. Then I knew I could at last look, look at that man of mine and back through our life together. What makes a lasting marriage, one that can take two disparate people and link them, in love and hate, inexorably together, the key of the padlock being long lost? My vision might be superficial at first, and I knew that only in time might subtleties emerge. But even now I must review as if I were an onlooker. So, at one remove I told myself the story.

A man married a maid and for each it was the first overwhelming passionate love. He tall, powerful, domineering; she shy, overprotected, and purely and passively feminine. And so eminently suitable a union! Both of the same general social, cultural, intellectual, educational, religious, financial, political, ethnic, and ethical backgrounds. So the pair lived happily forever and ever?

Six weeks after the wedding the maid knew how deeply a consuming passion could betray. Hers had been a flash fire that had consumed itself. Ashes only were left and all one long summer night she sifted these ashes through her fingers in her mind and looked into the dark of the years ahead.

And so began a marriage: he who had never used a tool or challenged his mind, she who was uncreative and had never cooked a meal or seen a dirty diaper. Steadily more and more differences emerged. He, an only child, was chained to his mother out of fear of her anger and scorn; she, the frail one of four siblings, was linked to her mother by invisible bonds that allowed no escape: spidery, cobwebby bonds of such tender love and empathy and intuition no thought of anger or resistance had chance of access to her mind.

He was city bred, judgmental, trained to a superficial and rigid social conformity that she thought of at first as the brave new world; she was country reared, in touch with nature, modest, self-effacing, and totally naive.

He panicked if he mislaid keys, wallet, or cigarette lighter. Everything waited breathless till they were found. His training in folding his clothes at night had been incredibly high. She left things in a disorder that drove him wild, but she had complete faith in the knowledge that lost things always turned up eventually, and if they didn't, by then it didn't matter. He mowed grass in perfectly straight lines, turning neatly at the end of a row. She cut swiftly in great circles.

He wanted no children; she wanted a lot, and since in his love he could deny her nothing, she achieved four. She was emotional, impulsive, intense, and apt to have ailments when not childbearing. Self-analytical, she tried to be compassionate of others by the same means, understanding. He never mentioned physical pain, never complained if ill, would not speak of feelings and disliked having them discussed.

He could enjoy hurting people, sometimes verbally, sometimes physically with his powerful handshake, smiling grimly at the wince he could feel. Once only he hurt her.

She said, "No! Please, darling! You'll lose me if you ever do that again!" Her gestures and words were always designed to soothe and placate. She could not deliberately step on an ant.

He wanted only the daily bread of emotional peace and freedom from anxiety. The new frightened him. She needed excitement to override her inner turmoil. He often punished the children severely if she was absent. Technically she stood by him but afterward comforted the child tenderly, her heart in conflict, thereby creating confusion.

Having started work in her family's textile firm after business school, he remained there for forty years, doing routine work and generally inadequate because he did not have the mental flexibility required in that volatile field, hating his job yet afraid to change. She began to want adventure: anything new, any mental challenge.

Where she was afraid to hate or even be angry at anyone lest they reject her, he cared nothing about being liked or loved by anyone but her. A few people did not care to come to the house.

Was there ever a raised voice? His could be strong, powerful, hers pleading.

Generally away from the children. But hate and anger and bitterness that could sizzle underneath were slept out by him at night just as they were written out by her at the same time in her notebook of the moment. And always a new day began.

As the children left one by one there was no collapse as in some marriages where it is only the offspring that hold a pair together. There was deep relief at a job being over, relief from distractions and multiple personalities and crises and those jealousies that had fostered a sense of being split emotionally. And now they could begin their own development within their chosen directions. And each aided and abetted the other and the bonds of caring grew strong.

For they learned gradually to labor together as both developed new skills. She never trained herself to use tools, but was quick to hand him the right one before he asked for it. He projected her mural designs onto the areas she was decorating, and erected her scaffolds. Together they built granite walls and terraces; he with a lever, she with chucks . . . until he tried to play Archimedes with a monster boulder and she, half under it, had enough sense to draw the line. She chose, he carried home, both together polished and mounted, fine bits of driftwood, and Mrs. Art and Mr. Craft sold these natural sculptures.

Like a stream around a dam, his expressiveness found its own channels, and she egged him on to tell his best stories and eventually to act in amateur productions. (He was most memorable in the touching comedy, Death Takes a Holiday, *so tall and stern in his black cape lined in red.)*

Home became a contentment of achievement. Insensibly each absorbed some of the other's strengths, he gaining courage, she patience and discretion. They had found out, without overt communication, how much each needed to be loved, and, even more important, how to give the unstinting love needed by the other. And so they bonded triumphantly. And of course the children watched the dance.

And thus it was, finally, that my telescopic view of our marriage reaffirmed what I had known before, that never was a woman as blindly and devotedly and forgivingly adored as I by my Alec and why I could never have hurt him willingly. And I saw that we had been true and courageous survivors, and had learned to fill our cage with song.

Late in June came a funny little incident. While driving on a two-lane road one day, I found myself slowed to about twenty m.p.h. by a line of cars ahead. One dreadfully poky driver was holding us up. Car after car, seeing a bit of straightaway, gunned and rushed past. Finally I was directly behind, to wait my chance. The offending car was ancient and in it were two white heads, one male, one female, so low in the seats that age must have shrunken them badly. Then I noticed their vanity plate. OLD MAN. How wonderful! They were evidently satisfied with their state, announcing it, and feeling their right to drive as it suited them. I no longer wanted to pass; I felt they had found a freedom and an amusement in life that fed into contentment. Was my sense of humor coming back? My amusement had no wryness: I felt mirthful, tolerant . . . tickled.

Soon I moved into full swing again, looking out, not in. Now everything was a "first time," not the old "last time." Though there was occasional sheet lightning on my horizon, none touched down to strike, and the few distant rumbles of emotional storm were hardly noticed.

In July my heart spoke. Authoritatively.

Loudly. "Move!" I hadn't even contemplated it before. Now I knew to a certainty that I would not face another winter in that place, deeply though Alec and I had loved the house we had lived and worked in for twenty-five years. Its size, the responsibility, the isolation, and the hazards of the road all had made their statement. Within twenty-four hours I gave a down payment on a nearly finished condominium only two miles away, on one level and in deep woods, close to a pond. When I told the children, they groaned and grieved. Though they had never lived in the old house, they saw it as the place of our togetherness.

Now I became intensely busy, taking on two widows' groups, one short-term, one long-, and learning the subtleties of family therapy, a fairly new form of treatment that required still another use of self in practice. And I was clearing out, step by step, the accumulated clutter of our house; polishing up brasses and furniture to make the new start a shining one, and working on a book for family consumption.

Aside from a few technical articles done in collaboration, I had never written "formally" before—only an insomniac's midnight notes, a few tight, yearning little verses and an unacceptable novel, before psychoanalysis began to set free my imagination. This full-length book concerned Bay View—a stretch of Cape Ann coastline where a cluster of family cottages had sprung up around my great-grandfather's mansard-roofed summer house. A poor student in school and college—too shy and tight, and unhandy with some symbols almost to the point of dyslexia—I now enjoyed doing research into local history, ordering topics into a logical flow, reconciling conflicting records. Before Alec's death, I'd collected memorabilia and written bits of reminiscence. Now they found their place in an extended survey of my family.

In December, almost a year to the day of Alec's death, the moment came to move to my small, comfortable new house. Most of the children could help on that Saturday, and so efficiently did they work together that by Sunday night everything was in order, even pictures hung. What a wild two days! "No party this year," I said, knowing they'd understand. "Just checks." My daughter and her family gave me a quiet, relaxed Christmas Day at their house. And I easily—well, fairly easily—gave the blue dressing gown to Alec Junior. I no longer had to have it. But I thought of the pain that follows any death and I knew I was changed, for deep grief can anneal or destroy, and I found myself caught in the universal angst of mourning. I was grieving, in a way, for the dead of every war, every famine, every natural calamity, but in no way could I grasp the enormity of emotional suffering in all of the members of all of the families of all of the dead. Everywhere, too much! Too much! I must busy myself again and forget.

In the almost two decades since my mother's death my mind had turned to her only occasionally, but always softly, tenderly, and compassionately. Now should I slowly and surely do the same with my loss of Alec. He too must become the bittersweet memory that evolves from resolved grief.

CHAPTER 6

The year 1976 became 1977. My new house was in pristine order and I began, like any animal, to sniff out my boundaries—first the immediate neighborhood, then every path to the limits of the ample acres of Conservation land within which we lay. But I reconnoitered alone. Snoopy, alas, alas, was expendable and so was expended before I moved.

Though dogs were permitted, the few there were seemed to be staid, rheumatic and elderly and were supposed to be leashed. Snoopy, like Gretchen, like all of that inbred breed, was over-protective, jealous and intense. Let any other dog step on the land of our old house and he, transformed into a vicious little white mass at high torque, flung himself upon the trespasser; his enormous pointed canines, fine for killing foxes, sank through fur to a hard flesh grip, and mighty then were the sounds of battle. How could I teach him to recognize the mere forty feet of frontage that was his to protect? And dogfights are one thing I fear deeply.

Extended search had turned up no one person, no place, to take a dog of Snoopy's age. But oh, my shame and my conscience! I could not, would not, take him to the vet's myself. A loving friend offered and Snoopy jumped happily into her front seat and as they went I wept tears that belonged to Alec, wept for life that goes, wept at deliberately causing a death, wept because Snoopy had transferred his fealty and love from Alec to me. And now I . . . I could see just how that little dog, trembling with delicious excitement, would strain at the leash to get into that waiting room where all the wonderful dog smells were. . . .

My neighbors, I found, were good people, mostly couples who had given up larger houses as their children moved away—the "post-nesters"—and it seemed that they wanted their privacy even as did I. Result: friendliness and kindness and physical proximity, a warm greeting every time you stepped out, yet never, ever, any intrusion or overt curiosity about you. One neighbor, whose condominium was about a hundred feet from mine, went to work every day only a little later than I did. His CB handle was "Fly," so when we were lucky Fly and Antique Beaver enjoyed a morning chat until distance diminished our voices to a blur.

In general it was a good year, a proud year, a creative year in that I was keeping busy and useful. The only signs that all was not well were increasing fatigue in my back and numbness in my left leg. A low-grade worry, my back always reminding me of the ugly iron scoliosis brace of adolescence, from shoulders to thighs, straps under armpits and between legs—a form of torture with the sense of being bound like a Chinese woman's feet. I couldn't run free like my cousins. The brace came off eventually, but backaches during childbearing required me to wear a heavy corset; and after that I lived with a come-and-go back weakness, so that I became accustomed to it and learned to massage it at night with a crooked right elbow. Then I had two accidents in midlife, one a cracked vertebra, undiagnosed for months of pain and treated with bed rest, and another brace, until further X-rays disclosed the fracture, which was put right with a laminectomy; the second, a boating accident, produced complications which required several operations in several years.

But why should my back become troublesome now with everything going so well? At work I kept muscles in slight motion by rocking gently in my loosened desk chair, and after a while began keeping my left leg elevated. Staff and clients accepted my oddities with equanimity, but in spite of satisfaction at work and contentment in my new home, the year 1977 began to take on an anxious, precarious quality.

In the summer a psychiatrist friend offered me some Colombian marijuana and a delightfully tiny pipe, obtained by one of his daughters. Though I had smoked about two and a half packs of cigarettes a day for over forty years, I had never willingly or wittingly inhaled. There was a well-established mental block between the smoke and my lungs. My friend knew that cannabis eased pain, induced sleep, and should be legal for prescription by doctors. The initiation was bad, however. I coughed, choked and sputtered.

"Suck in, don't blow out!"

"I can't help it."

"Try again, now, inhale."

"But I'm swallowing the smoke."

"Hold your nose then. Here, I'll hold it. Now draw in. Breathe deeply."

"It hurts."

Then my friend took the pipe and tried it for himself for the first time in his fifty-odd years. He coughed and we laughed and laughed.

But I had found that one good inhalation of the smoke had the effect, within a few minutes, of deepening my breathing, relaxing my body, reducing pain sharply, and putting me almost immediately to sleep while I mused vaguely over swift mental pictures and thoughts that were not associated in any way with one another, and which literally floated me off. I also found that my stern and sometimes angry conscience was easing. This was a new freedom for me, a benefit of aging. And it was amusing to mention casually (if selectively) that I smoked pot, and to watch the quick start of incredulity. Yet I used the stuff more and more rarely. I might break the nation's law comfortably in such areas now but I never really won against family orders as passed down, "Never take anything noxious into your body, and particularly anything that can affect your mind." Long since has the little pipe rested among my curios. But it was a very kind friend for a while.

Christmastime rolled in predictably. I wanted it to be the best one ever. Two years before was Alec's death with the holiday being merely a vague remote event. The following year, having just moved, I held a family gathering to be merry but in reality saying, "Behold me and my new home—both doing well." But there were no presents from the heart. I did send a very few Christmas cards I found in a museum catalog, to closest friends and relatives. At the time the card seemed delightfully whimsical and eminently suitable. A black silhouette on unrelieved white of a proud lady driving a pung behind a spirited horse. Her head is high, as is her steed's; reins and whip expertly guide his spanking pace. Her back is arched. So is his. Both look swift, smart, and superior. Again I was saying, "See, so soon after Alec's death and I am in control."

This year, however, I would give magnificently of my house, my soul, and my possessions to my descendants.

My memories of Christmas were never of pure delight. Indeed, the first was of absolute misery. When the nearby grandparents came with their presents, my older brother got a train set, my younger an Indian tent, my sister (one and one-half years my senior) got a great, great beautiful golden-curled, pink-ruffled doll with moving eyes, while I got—a teddy bear. Hate and rage and bitterness exploded in me. And the second memory was of panic. When I was six or seven—and I remember my white muslin party dress with the big shoulder ruffles—in a moment of time after the tapers on the tree were lighted but no one was in sight, I sneaked in and bent to peer beneath the tree to view my important name on some gift. My ruffles touched flame, my dress flared, and I ran (I suppose screaming) toward the door. An uncle, entering, put out the fire—with hands? a rug?—and almost at once I, scared but quite unhurt and squeezing myself into the corner of the lowest step of the front hall stairs, found myself proffered and opening a quickly selected and special present—my first watch—the while I was aware of the worried faces watching me.

For years, after all gifts were opened and papers were strewn around, I still searched among them and deep in the spruce branches for some special tiny box for me that I was sure had been mislaid. Later still, with naive confidence, I headed my Christmas list "Packard Runabout" (like my uncle's car which, at twelve, I was just learning to drive on the isolated country roads, peering through the steering wheel instead of over it). Yes, I was innocently greedy, and home presents were, by necessity, frugal, mostly clothes and books. The family's rule was caution, abstention, and respect for the intrinsic worth of even the most trivial article until it was worn out.

My father's cousins used to tease me by calling me "the still pig." I resented this bitterly knowing well the old adage, "The still pig gets the swill." I only half recognized that by being good, gentle, obedient, and wistful I could reap well. And I counted on my indulgent bachelor uncle's occasional impulses to play fairy godfather. My hopes of him brought magic to the possibilities of Christmas Day.

With marriage came our own Christmas, but no fulfillment came with it. Our customs had to be in the ways of, and usually at the house of, Alec's mother and father. And I at once discovered that Alec hated Christmas. In time I insisted on my ways for the children's enjoyment, but learned to be very low-key in my shopping or in discussing it. Even wrapping presents I usually did while he was asleep. I involved him each year, however, through the necessity of his building a stand for the tree, and slowly he got more tolerant. But right after our big noon meal the tree had to be dedecorated and deracinated and put outside, the ornaments repacked and removed to the attic, the floor vacuumed. Only then could he relax.

It was a great relief to know eventually just why that silent man so hated the day. In an unprecedented recall of early memory he told me how . . .

He loved peanuts. He was little. He was getting ten cents allowance a week, but five cents had to go into the plate at church where, every Sunday, he was made to sit through the full service and no wiggling. The other five cents was his own. He always spent it on peanuts in their shells. He loved peanuts very much. One Sunday he only pretended to put the nickel in the plate. His mother spotted two bags of peanuts in his jacket pockets and forced out of him (he couldn't remember how) a confession. It was just before Christmas. She openly declared a day of mourning, returned presents to friends and relatives and stores, took down all ornaments, let the maids go home for a holiday, and then took herself, husband, and son to a small almost empty country inn, and all Christmas Day she sat and stared at Alec and never uttered a word. Just stared. "How old?" I asked. "Six or seven, I think." Oh, poor little boy! I too had experienced a bit of that grim cold expressionless stare. Alec's memory may have distorted the picture. My telling of it may have. But the fear in Alec could never be erased.

For years his presents to me were a Phillips Brooks calendar and perhaps a box of paper clips. Imagination was totally absent. Decades later someone introduced him to the men's Christmas Club at Bonwit Teller's. That was a different story. He drank the free martinis, he picked out the gorgeous female figure nearest, in his eyes, to mine, he watched her model this and that, and he came home late bearing the golden boxes with their lingerie treasures. Money no object. When he retired we were back to the

Phillips Brooks calendars again. After thirty or forty years I glued, yearly, a brightly colored picture over Phillips Brooks's bland kind face. I'd looked at the Reverend Mr. Brooks long enough.

Slowly and surely I learned that in marriage dependency availed me nothing but that being depended upon made our merry-go-round of marriage and children work. And I found that it was the giving, not the getting, that made the fire glow. But also I learned, at a belated last, to say firmly and strongly, after Christmas dinner was over and the kitchen reordered, that *nobody* was to ask *anything* of me the rest of the day. I knew inside that I had momentarily run dry. For I had bought, wrapped, hidden, given; persuaded and pretended, seduced, hugged, comforted; cooked, and cleaned up, and had opened the children's small gifts and slowly learned the glory that could lie behind them and their simple offering.

But something always *was* missing. Those Christmases *were* inhibited by anxiety over Alec's comfort and his dislike of seeing a lot of his descendants at once—all too plainly expressed: he could never remember his grandchildren's names. I liked my all-doing, all-giving role, yet there was my nagging, unfulfilled—and guilty—need to *get*.

Now it was altogether gone. Nineteen seventy-seven would be our first real family Christmas, and I anticipated it as a kind of sacrament. The unalloyed pleasure of giving cast a glow over my weeks of preparation.

The last two presents were the most awkward, treasures long coveted by the children, that now after a year in the new house were proven expendable. One, acquired in the Philippines on a freighter trip we had enjoyed in a respite between my back operations, was an enormous and very old brass gong some two feet across. It fought both me and the wrapping paper, but was finally mastered and secured. The other, a fine set of antique fireplace accessories with their heavy stand, also meant bending, stretching, and reaching, and I was fresh out of that motion. I struggled. My back grabbed at me. I suddenly knew the shock in my sacroiliac area. I felt the trauma spread over me like a blackout. Up my back, over my shoulders, down to my coccyx, across my buttocks until I was immobilized.

Later the fireplace accessories went into an old commercial laundry bag to join the other presents in their gaudy trimmings. But I was in total disarray. Concealment was possible only from the younger generation. My children understood and said nothing.

CHAPTER 7

After three weeks in the hospital in January, where practically everything done for backs and spasms was tried and brought no relief, after being politely kicked out because the hospital needed the bed for the more acutely ill, after a week at home, I returned to work. My clients were getting anxious. Besides, what else was there to do? Sit home and fry in my own intense discomfort and frustration? My lower back could not distinguish between its own burning and the stinging of the electric bed pad turned up too high. My body, in its rigidity, was so frozen it allowed no single free motion.

In April my doctor told me I'd have to learn to live with pain. I accepted the challenge—what else could I do?—with a grim determination and a stepped-up level of activity that led inevitably to exhaustion.

After the passing of a spring during which I neither heard nor saw the renewal of life, and finally, in June, after a sudden realization that I no longer could lose myself in concern and involvement with the needs of those I was treating, I resigned. It gave me a grim satisfaction that the clinic head urged me to take any necessary leave of absence and then come back. But I declined; I needed to hide and lick my wounds for a long time.

During the next month came the bitter task of transferring my cases to other workers. It had to be done. It had to be done with caring and tenderness.

The last day at the office was in mid-July. I cleaned up my desk, putting plants, pictures, dictating machine, and sundry in the car. For the last time I went in to our Family Therapy seminar. We were a very close group and we were all feeling sad. One asked, "What will you do now? Being you, you can't do nothing." I said lightly, "Seek wisdom. That's what retirement's for." But it was all too much. I realized I had just used the word *retirement* for the first time.

I left abruptly. At home I locked the door, turned off the telephone, swallowed Valium and codeine, and got undressed. I was suddenly old, an old woman, retired. Old, bedridden, and in chronic pain! Until my death? Up to now I had managed to keep myself benignly unaware of my age, and the attitudes at work and among my many younger friends had fostered my avoidance.

But now, old! Old was illness and anxiety and fears and insecurity; stupidity and flatness of emotion; depression and despair; constriction of brain, blood vessels, and lungs; anility and anality. Wasn't it? In my nightgown I sat on the side of my bed and thought. For years I had not looked in a mirror except to check my hair or see that my slip didn't show. What had I been denying? Drawing a deep breath, looking fear in the face, I stood stark naked before the long mirror. For decades I hadn't focused on my physical self. Now I saw time's toll: drooping breasts, large flabby belly, spread hips, pendulous flesh on my upper arms, bowed shoulders, swayback. I pinched myself; the flesh went only slowly back to place. And there were all those scars from my many surgical mutilations. Must I feel again, not only pain and fear, but humiliation, and the shamed diffidence of the homely iron-harnessed bucktoothed adolescent I had once been? And my face? Wrinkled, old, a large dark keratosis by one eye I couldn't be bothered to have removed, and my expression—sour!

Upon that mirror image I superimposed my figure of late adolescence, after the brace had straightened it out: slim, tall, long straight legs, silky flesh, youth in full bloom; but I also remembered how even then I had longed for curly hair and bigger breasts and a wider mouth, which, I was told, stood for generosity of spirit. My fantasy at that time was of being the greatest courtesan in France—infinitely rare, wise, enchanting, desirable, seductive, yet adored forever by every man she left for her next great amour. Sex, somehow, didn't enter into it. How silly could a flapper be?

Or an old lady? As I stood there, amusement rose within me, that old age should have caught me by surprise, and my face changed before my eyes, alight, not dour. And a moment hung in air—I had a choice—would I take it? I could go on cringing for the rest of my life or I could live. Alec always saw my body as he had seen it fifty years before—desirable and beautiful and touchable, for love does that. Even just prior to his death, what more artistically exquisite than my seventy-nine-year-old husband's hands, strong, knobbed, with blue veins showing through; hands that had done physical things with delicacy or tremendous power. And his face, deeply lined from the conflicts of a temperament that was capable of great swings between passion—even violence—and tenderness, was a study in bone structure and character. Well, I had what I had for physical capital—mine own and therefore precious in an earthy way, and my skin was still silky. The old woman in the mirror laughed again. Old, and so be it. And so to bed.

I woke to my seventy-eighth birthday. And now my body dictated my days. Here was my house, my bedroom, my bed, the table full of books. Here was I, half propped up, large pillow under my knees, heating pad at my back. Down the hall was the little kitchen. Morning. Breakfast in bed. Coffee, fruit, raisin bran or granola if I had any appetite. Noon. Lunch, usually crackers and cheese with maybe a gin and tonic or a bloody mary—everything minimum effort, minimum standing. Bed. Midafternoon, after nap, pre-preparation for supper. I sit at the kitchen table to fix a vegetable. Back to bed. Late afternoon. Return to get ready whatever protein appealed—meat, fish, eggs—set the supper tray. Back to bed. At six, pour a drink. Back to bed to go on reading. Night. The outside world through the media penetrated but faintly, its stridency exhausting, its disarray and speed too distracting.

Every couple of hours my body needed to move and I wandered around, to get something, replace something, realign something, water a plant or two. Then back to bed. Once in a while I strolled a little way outside, praying I would meet no one. That summer I sat out on my deck but not for long. I could not get comfortable. Back to bed. And always pain, pain!

But though my body ruled my physical days, must my mind crawl too? Not unless I gave up. The mind, I found, like nature, abhors a vacuum. Undirected now, it worked like a disturbed hill of ants. How *did* old people handle degeneration, dissolution, and their future meeting with death?

Once started I read avidly on aging, books soon coming from all directions. What else was there to do? Read and think and read again. Memories flooded in, apt comparisons came to mind, insights broke through. Time to think was something new to me. In childhood daydreaming or looking absentminded was discouraged; in marriage it was my "going away" that Alec feared. Only at night, while he slept, could I take out my notebook, but under the personal and professional pressure of those years I could seldom sort out ideas from emotions. I was free now. But anger rose in me, anger for (and at!) all the depressed old I was learning more about, for those in pain, in fear, in poverty, in substandard nursing homes, or, like myself, trapped in their own beds and their own futility. Is there anything more deadly than endless pain and frustration? By day I waited for the night to come. At night I waited for the day.

Insomniac since childhood, I knew that sleeping drugs are depressants, can lead to habituation, and that the normal sleep cycle, with its REM (dreaming) sleep can thereby be so distorted that the body does not get its restorative rest. I still took the pills. I knew that five to seven hours of sleep is plenty for people my age. Not for me! I needed much more time of oblivion, so tired were my body and brain. Common sense told me not to worry but to get busy at something that distracts the mind. Nothing did. Or to drink some warm milk, which is a soporific; I hate warm milk. And I knew that if I once wondered if I would be able to drop off to sleep, I certainly wouldn't. So most nights, as I lay quietly with my lids closed, the wide-eyed alertness and intensity went on. It was like a cloudless, moonless sky when the air is so pellucid every star crackles. Yet nothing stirred. I had no specific thoughts. If this went on for hours, I had learned to look for some hidden anger, so subtle and so denied it was almost impossible to recognize.

Lots of us put a mask on in youth and wear it for the rest of our waking lives. But it comes off in the dark, in serious illness and finally, for good, at death. The trouble is that in the dark of the night the dark of the soul stirs. We know its actions only as a tension and a restlessness, a body that aches or is not relaxed, a mind that races through the day past or the day to come. Perhaps our skin may itch, our legs may keep twitching, we may ache. (Though I am told that the jerk or jump of a muscle as one begins to drowse is actually the sudden letting go of tautness in that area.) There may be some long-gone worry or some long-in-the-future dread, a sense of gloom or despair, or, particularly nasty, a tiny seed of resentment at someone, and on that we can build, step by step; we escalate, gather in, aggrandize, until we are almost burning with a now completely righteous rage and rationale for hate.

There are many names for what besets us—Devil, the Unconscious, the Demon—and each tribe, each primitive race or religion or philosophy, has its own. They are all one; an expression of our instinctual life: the potential evil and the potential creativeness within us. But we are afraid; afraid of the blackness of the night and the bleak blackness of our soul; afraid of seeing ourselves naked without the cultural consciousness of our particular race; afraid of our wish to kill, to devour, to maim and torture; afraid of our hate and vindictiveness; afraid of a devouring love (given or received), of violent retaliation, of abandonment, of intolerable suffering, of the prelude to death. And we are afraid of death, and in a curious way afraid of our own fear. And finally we are afraid of the utter inner loneliness that is the lot of man.

As a sleepless child, I tried prayer, but "Now I lay me down to sleep" always suggested fearful death. "Our Father who art in heaven" seemed to feed me nothing.

"The Lord is my shepherd" sometimes quieted my tense body if I repeated it very slowly. (I never mentioned those lonely hours to my mother. She may have guessed. She knew altogether too much about me.) My religious training had been almost nonexistent. I don't remember ever hearing the word *God* uttered in our family except once. That was on a sharply clear August night when mother led me out to the field where the soft rowan was ready for cutting, and we lay on our backs and looked up at the moonless sky; the stars so many, so twinkly, so brilliant, and she talked softly of the vastness of the universe and of how there might be a God but no one could ever know, and how Christ was a rare and compassionate man in a troubled and wicked time, but no true son of God. Yet we should try to live our lives as close to his precepts as we could. "Our Father" and the twenty-third Psalm I learned in grade school.

I remember no challenging religious discussions in college. The few friends I achieved in four years were almost as simpleminded and literal as I. I knew only of an anthropomorphic God, a person, not a concept, from our maids, who were usually young Irish girls. And I foreswore Him the night our first child was born. I was still babe-innocent in every way. I was staying with my in-laws in the city, utterly ignorant of the process to come, and fearful. When the water broke, I asked Alec to call Mother, who had planned to come in from the country to be with me in the hospital, just as her mother had come to her. Mrs. Robey (who had nearly died giving birth to Alec) turned on me like a tigress. "I never heard such selfishness! I knew you always thought of yourself first. To ask your mother to come this far at night just for you! Alexander, I forbid you to call her!"

I learned only later that it was an exceptionally swift birth for a first baby, both easy and violent, for it occurred while the nurse, having established me in the hospital bed, went to report to the doctor and Alec that it would be some hours' wait. In her absence incredible powers moved into my body, and my stomach, bowels, bladder and uterus all rejected what they contained under one great spasm of thrust. The horror was unspeakable since soiling was the worst of shames. And I knew a fear such as I never knew again. And I prayed; I cried out to Him. Nothing! Again. Nothing! And the nurse was there now, forcing back with all her strength the emerging baby's head. Never again would I cry out for deep comfort. I could not risk rejection.

And now, fifty-five years later, old, invalided, with father, mother, Alec gone, I had to be my own sick child. I was not about to search for God, let alone think about Him. Was I not still angry? Or was it anger at an implacable mother who once, perhaps just once, refused succor, would not open her door to her screaming child. I could remember nothing. But like some griefs of childhood my rage knew no reason.

Until I was about five I was adventurous, saucy and pert, flirtatious, determined, and jealous and had temper tantrums when thwarted. But after five, I took on a powerful conscience and became shy, timid, and too good. Not one of the dozens of snapshots taken and preserved by mother and my spinster aunt showed me with anything but a completely solemn, even a sad, face; never so much as a half-smile.

I was almost forty before I found I had a tiger, tiger burning bright within my preciousness. It occurred one day in an analytic session. I was rigid and restless and the doctor remarked, "You're pretty knotted up with anger and hate, aren't you?"

I hit the ceiling. "I've *never* hated anyone in my life. Never! I'm *never* angry."

"No?"

There was long silence, full of implications. Then I burst into tears. He handed me, finally, a box of Kleenex. The good, loving, pure, innocent, child-girl-woman had melted away. I saw that I had been one great lie, playing a role most of my life. I could feel a sudden loss of self, the self I had built up so carefully through the years.

That wide-eyed night, panic came. Alec slept quietly. Blind and bewildered, I stood in the middle of the room like an animal at bay. Then the door frame in dim light drew me. I moved slowly toward it and touched it. Should I smash my head against it? It was solid—solid and perpendicular. I ran my hand up and down the jamb and thought, "It's real. I feel. Therefore I still *am*. I am! Hold on to that!" I rubbed my fingers over a little roughness in the paint. I leaned my head against that door and went still for a long time. Then I got into bed again. Tomorrow would come. What does one do with a nobody for a self?

The emotional pain of near dissolution of the self is by definition weird and frightening and not easily forgotten. I've been told that once one finally loses all contact with or awareness of reality and is institutionalized, pain eases, for one now *is* a nobody to oneself yet doesn't know it. It is the slow coming back to normality again that hurts, for now there can be shame added to the previous conflicts.

Gradually, after I looked at and worked on my angers at Alec, at his mother (one could never be angry at his mild father), at my father (solely because I thought he preferred my sister to me), after I looked at frustrations and hurt feelings and bitterness, all so in-sealed heretofore, some even decades heretofore, after I found my anger and hate didn't kill either me or any other person, the time came when I was able to look timidly at my relationship with Mother. There was never anything specific you could put your finger on to be annoyed at with her. (Only once. She had promised to have a new doll's dress finished when I got back from school. I ran upstairs to her. She hadn't even touched it.) In her frequent bouts of neuralgia I always brought her tray to bed, and picked, in season, a flower or a bright leaf for the tray to win her smile. We were closest during each other's illnesses.

Then after one of my therapeutic hours came a dream of her killing me. Totally unable to tolerate the terror that rose in me in my desire to retaliate, at my primal rage, I plunged into depression. And that has its own particular pain of no-pain. I recall one of my children running to me crying. The other three followed as usual to see what Mother would do or say. I sat there utterly unfeeling, looking vaguely from one face to another. Then I got into the car and drove toward the ocean I so loved. It was a wild day, the cold rain slatting, the wind landward. I left the car and went to the edge of the rocks. Slowly, bit by bit, I moved down closer and closer to where the huge waves crashed up, flinging their spray, then sucking down before the surge and impact of the next. Closer, closer. I was not thinking suicide. I was not thinking anything. I was, dimly, absorbed with that power.

Suddenly an inner voice called. "Go home! Go home!" I did, the car crawling, my foot too limp to press the accelerator firmly, my mind numb. Such things are hard on children, but at least I did come back. And Dr. Y brought me through nicely.

For a while, in some strange vision, I saw my anger as totally destructive to others, as a great slimy evil hateful aborted loathsome excrescence, destroying and feeding on all it touched and all that touched it, growing wildly out of control, a true cancer. How to make my daylight mind surround this sickness, absorbing it slowly for my self-preservation? It would always be in my body, but could I not keep it contained?

My Tiger of William Blake's poem, which spoke to the violence of those unconscious instincts in the dark of the soul, slowly became quite acceptable. For years I had a poster on the wall of my office, just behind the heads of my clients but where I could see it. I had found that bit of serendipity in a closing-out sale, and it pictured a tiger in brilliant oranges and clean blacks, a beast who is lurking, prowling in the night, mouth wide, great teeth bared, eyes glaring and staring, whiskers bristling, every claw extended. A full moon glowed orange in the background. But gradually the cruel bared teeth took on a similarity to a grin—sometimes leering, sometimes amused and friendly. Occasionally a client was disturbed by the picture, but its implications usually wove in well with the work we were doing. And in the afternoons my office was used for play therapy with children, but none of them (I was told when I asked) were bothered by it. One new little girl stared at the tiger, fascinated and absorbed, and thereafter she always insisted on playing in that room where she could see her "nice kitty."

My inner tiger is no kitty, but somewhere along the line I've made friends with him and he and I can grin back at each other. If he leaps out at me it is usually only a moment of fear before I see the amusement in his eye and can laugh at myself for my reaction. Not all of the time. Most of the time.

Lucky or not, blessed are those whose faith in their God is unwavering. "My misery is His will. I bow my head. He alone knows how weak and little and fallible I am. He loves me." For these, do ardent prayers reduce the Tiger burning bright to a kitty?

For me, some days, thinking seemed like dynamite, with no way to snuff out the fuse that would glow and sputter until I became senile or too depressed to feel. I couldn't stop it, and I couldn't divert it from myself. And for some reason depression didn't come to me, or I wasn't aware of it. Only intense anxious restlessness. So I tried out TV, rarely looked at before. I ordered a small colored set with remote control and had it placed about four feet from my bed, and I watched it like any other old lady, finding it wonderful and terrible. I could see that the soap operas would be a daily pleasure for those who gain a little time of Lethe by viewing the human comedy in its pathos and bathos, at its sentimental noblest and vilest; that angry old people might let out a little of their own inner turmoil in programs of violence (fairy stories for adults); that Lawrence Welk would bring back to some the old, happy memories. He was so pleasantly the same, week in and week out, and so would become a symbol of longevity. The talk shows had MCs who could be idols of a kind, always dependable, reasonably clean-spoken even when a participant got out of hand, kindly father figures for the old. Finally the game shows could be a vicarious adventure if one could follow the complexities. It was from the Public Broadcasting Service only that I got any pleasure. But I couldn't avoid commercials at news time.

For us old people, the universe is what the media choose to show us. And the ugly areas of life about which we can do nothing as individuals are the ones they love; every detail of wars, murder, assassinations, bombings, hijackings, plane crashes, hold-ups, catastrophic fires and earthquakes, jail breaks, fatal auto accidents, arson and rape, battering, and muggings.

I—we, I thought irritably—know quite enough of the evil in humanity. We've gone through all the rites of passage but one, death, and we're fairly canny old birds. Most of us have endured four wars, which hurt us, Prohibition, which taught us to drink, the stock market crash, which scared us, and the Great Depression, which showed us the beauty of a dime. We've voted for ten, twelve, fourteen, even sixteen Presidents and innumerable federal, state, and local officials. We've read of the modern medical miracles that have saved our lives, though not necessarily what our lives are for. And the arms race? Maybe the world might be the better for being blown up to let new forms of life make a fresh start. We know all too well the anguish entailed in each injury and death and we ourselves are not personally immune to natural disasters, potential mugging, vandalism, thefts, fire, or even rape.

But one thing moved me to utmost irritation. If our aging bodies didn't make us constantly aware of ourselves, the question-and-answer medical programs, the endless articles in papers and magazines on diets, illnesses, any and every symptom whatever would remind us again and again of our own fragility and mortality. And with what fiendish skill do advertisements attack those body parts we learned as children to see as unattractive, which are even more unattractive to us now that we are old; oily or dandruffy hair, nasal drip, bad breath, slipping dentures, underarm perspiration, bloated stomach, vaginal odors, constipation and hemorrhoids and excess body hair. And then we, who have little appetite anyway, are shown enormous six-inch-high sandwiches, ingested with glittering eyes.

With what strange delight and gloom the media show new finding of products that prove to be carcinogenic. Saccharin banned, unbanned; swordfish banned, later unbanned. And so on, not excluding coffee. Most foods are doctored up for preservation or flavor or eye appeal. Air, water, certain meats, vegetables grown in impurity may be dangerous. Day after day. Carcinogenic. We watch for lumps, bleeding, unusual constipation or diarrhea, weight loss, or unaccountable fatigue.

We have been "medicalized" by government, health workers, books and articles and advertisements and above all the press, which trumpets statistics on the incidence of dire diseases or the horrible discoveries of new ones. Ivan Illich in his book *Medical Nemesis* shows how ready the news is to ensnare us and how ready we are to become entangled in fear. Cancer is always as latent in our minds as the virus is latent in our blood.

We know too much—and not enough—ever to feel quite secure. We hear exaggerated promises for each new wonder drug on the market and horror stories about those that have been used for years but are now found to be dangerous. We know that even the reliable drugs may have side effects. And if we experience odd symptoms such as dizziness, headaches, queasiness, palpitations, it may be only that the doctor, in prescribing, has forgotten to tell us what to anticipate. But it may be . . . *Something.*

Terror creeps in.

In those months of solitude and inward turning, any little ache or pain brought my mind upright to full salute. And if it did not subside (either the ache or my apprehension), I called my doctor for an appointment. It might be that symptom of *Something*. I am lucky enough, as many of the old are not, to have a regular doctor, a wise one, a fine one. He knows me, my personality, my nerves, my fears. With me, with all his patients, I imagine, he has a sixth sense of mind-body interaction. He has consistently given me compassionate warmth and wisdom, and it lights me up to have him visit me in a hospital even when I am under the care of a specialist. His fees are modest. And part of his smile belongs to me. Does he know how important he is to me?

So *Something* threatens, and I call. "No, not an emergency. Two weeks? Yes, I can wait." With cancer at the back of my mind, I watch the days. At last I am sitting in the waiting room—crowded, since several doctors practice here together. I watch the faces as they come and go: faces so impassive, so closed, I know these people too sense the worm of terror.

The nurse calls my name at last. I have a list of questions in my purse but forget to take it out. Oddly, I always become inarticulate in a doctor's presence. He examines, questions, and interprets my symptoms and what they mean in terms of what he already knows about me, but not in terms of the fears I don't manage to utter. And when I leave, maybe with a new prescription in hand, it is always, because of his smile, with some relief. He wouldn't smile if he'd seen something wrong; he wouldn't smile if he didn't care. But the smile doesn't mean he has thought of everything.

With a new doctor I am a sitting duck. He can't read me nor I him. And if I've been referred to a surgeon, I can't expect him to have any key to the infinitely varied subtleties of mind-body interaction and the games and subterfuges prompted by the subconscious. If my own doctor's wisdom can't solve the original problem, if his tests can't either, it is all too routine after that: consultation with a specialist, to be safe, to a hospital for further tests, to be safe, and on to the operating table, to be safe. And I always dread a further possibility, because it happened to me after that back injury on a boat: several more operations to correct an error made in the original one.

Yet I continue to see doctors first as gods and only second as fallible human beings. In social work, we have time, and the truth of a human situation eventually discloses itself. But a medicine man, who must decide on the spot, who may have intuition but is not trained in its use—and who may distrust or deny all that psychological "claptrap" anyway—what can he make of me, who am somehow unable to tell him what I feel and fear? "She says she hurts, and she does look drawn. Long history of surgery. Psychotherapy: that suggests an excitable, neurotic type. But she's certainly under control: natural composure? holding something in? depression? The record suggests functional elements at certain times; placebos never have helped, though. Exploratory surgery might turn up something."

Not only am I afraid of what he will decide; I am afraid of *how* he will decide. And I am afraid of the depersonalization of hospitals, and the loss of autonomy. And even of neglect. I have never been able to speak up and ask for what I want or need—only to try anxiously and silently to deserve it, by being good. But in hospitals, in any large impersonal institution, the crass old rule holds: the squeaky wheel gets the grease.

My upbringing was as powerful as it was impractical: I *cannot* "squeak." And I don't like it when my dressing gown meets another dressing gown in the corridor which is our walkway to recuperation. I'm not properly clad! I'm indecent! We strangers may be trundling along pieces of equipment, too, often quite unattractive and often unmistakable clues to quite unattractive ailments. In big city hospitals I hate being wheeled into, and out of, up, down, through, around, along endless alleys, passing or meeting the public from the outside world, who look idly or curiously at me. And it's worse now that my body is old and unlovely. I sympathize with the ladies of ancient China and the pretty "doctors' dolls" of carved ivory, on which they indicated the location of the pain in their own never-exposed bodies. I own one of these dolls and feel great fondness for it.

Though Alec had taught me, out of his love, to love my own body, my deep sense of privacy never had changed. I didn't heed my mother's warning, when I was just thirty-eight, that I must no longer wear sleeveless dresses. I didn't dress in my closet, as she did all her life, holding to her delicate Victorian purity and denying to the end the corruption that was body. But what is privacy but a need or a respect for distance between oneself and others?

Better the privacy of body than face? Some people are so afraid of emotional exposure they show little facial movement. Like their clothing, their expression is a mask.

During my professional years, unlike the average worker, I always put my clients in shadow, my own face to the light. I wanted them to see fully the echoes and vibrations of their words and emotions reflected in my own mobile expressions. It saved many words. I could read them even in shadow, for the body speaks, and they could read me—up to a point.

CHAPTER 8

It was taken for granted in my family that children loved their parents and each other and were loved in return. And as I must never feel hate, express rage, or show fear, I had no way of knowing that tigers are indigenous to the soil of the soul of man, and that even when caged their powers can be lethal. I gave up my temper tantrums early, but could not control my nightmares or my fears. So I hid them from myself by daydreams of nobility and courage, castles that grew in glory.

I was afraid of real things like dogfights and drunks and angry voices and tramps and, after the Christmas candle had caught my dress, fire. Even in my thirties I kept on trying to prove my valor to myself. For example, an emergency appendectomy was done under local anesthesia at my request; I watched the operation, reflected in the overhead mirrors, fascinated to see myself being cut up. But I preferred almost any amount of pain to the awful panic induced by ether, that dreadful sensation of being sucked into an endless whirlpool and of being totally out of control.

It has always saddened me to watch the desperate courage sometimes seen in children who rush into danger in hope of exorcism. I suspect some parents make unreasonable demands because they are numb with denial and so afraid of their own fear that they cannot tolerate it in their children. Was Mother really brave, or deathly afraid not to be? I remember when, with no help at hand, she drove a drunken tramp out of our house. Her calm voice was steely sharp with authority (but, clinging to her skirts, I felt her trembling).

There was the time, perhaps two years after my dress was burned, that our big chimney caught fire. The roar was terrible. Hurry! Hurry! Salt on the flames! Logs set in a pail and carried out! Father outside to watch the wind and see what sparks fell on the roof, getting out a ladder; older brother and sister holding a heavy rug against the fireplace opening to stop the draft. "You!

Harriet, quick. Go up into the crawl space above the boys' room, and crawl along to touch the chimney and see if the wood around it is on fire. Be terribly careful to put weight only on the beams, or you'll fall through to the floor below. Now hurry!" I hesitated. "Go!" came from Mother. "Go!" And I went, up two flights, down three steps to the old attic, climbed up on top of the water tank, and around the high and narrow metal-lined rim, on over a gap into that great dark hole, hand to strut, knee to strut, reaching out again and again in the inky dark, I went on, slower and slower to meet that roar ahead of me. At last I could touch cement, and it was hot, but there was no flame and no smoke. Hot, that was all. And the roar was subsiding. Back downstairs again, shaken, I found all had quieted from the earlier frantic haste, and Father reported almost no more sparks. But why, oh why, couldn't someone else have gone up into that hellhole?

One night (I was then perhaps sixteen), by chance I was entirely alone at our house on the shore. I had never been alone at night anywhere before, and as the evening wore on I became afraid, of rape or murder, or both. I went tensely to bed. It was in the little middle room upstairs, my room, in which the classic battle was fought out. I couldn't sleep. The horrors got worse and worse. Lights went out in all the houses around. I kept thinking of the open and inviting doors and windows downstairs. Finally, in despair, I went down and shut and locked every door and window, even those in the isolated living room. Now I would be safe. I went back to bed. A different type of struggle began, an internal one. Mother's face was with me, and her words "Never be afraid." At long last I made my decision simply and quickly, in some inexplicable way. I said, "Go!" to myself and went down again, unlocked and opened everything as it had been before, and felt the night breeze draw through. I even stood out on the porch for a very brief moment. Then I went up to my room and right to sleep.

Such experiences did not make me less timid, but I learned to cope with fear by denying it, which can be very useful though not enriching. It was as if my facade were made of bricks without mortar. And so, like many children brought up on counsels of perfection, always on trial and usually guilty, I fled my sense of inadequacy into a world of daydreams.

At first I was growing wings on my sharp, skinny shoulder blades, literally becoming an angel. No one realized, but when I had gone up to heaven they'd all be sorry. And a few years later I was heroic, a rescuer of those in danger (particularly at sea, my only athletic ability being swimming). My awards and rewards were enormous. Over and over I perfected the details. I didn't mature physically until very late, seventeen, which was when I became the most desirable courtesan in all France, the woman no man could ever forget. And for a short time after marriage I imagined doing fantastic things that would make Mrs. Robey respect and admire me, however grudgingly, forever.

Less farfetched were the ego ideals, the more realistic visions of the person I could try to be, the "perfect" wife and mother; a truly good woman, like my mother, obedient to all the family commandments, admired by all the clan. Additionally, she, I, would impress Mrs. Robey (reputed to be the best dinner partner in Boston) by sudden sophistication and knowledge of what was what. I'd had many lessons from that lady. When she received invitations, she always felt the envelope for the embossed mark of the stationers, of which there were apparently two acceptable ones in New York and three in Boston. (And in Boston, only one dressmaker—hers. She had my wedding dress made to her design. Mother had capitulated on many things to make the wedding go smoothly. I was not only pliant. I was impotent.)

I knew only one brief moment of personal glory. I was driving our Model T Ford home to the country one night after dinner with Alec's parents on Commonwealth Avenue. They, Alec, and two guests were seeing me out the front door, all still bemoaning my parents' laxness in allowing me to drive alone at night. I'd had enough. My fairy godfather uncle had given me, at sixteen, a revolver. Even though I rode only Rosy, the old carriage horse, who occasionally stumbled and fell with her weak knees (one time, to my fury, she lay on her side, totally relaxed, upper lip stretching to nibble at the grass of the roadside, and she wouldn't get up), I, in my adolescent daydreaming, longed to wear a revolver at my hip. So, there, then, in the Robeys' hall, I pulled the revolver from my coat pocket and tossed the lovely blue-gray shiny little Colt .24 from one hand to the other. They all stood in stunned silence as I went out the door in my bravest bravado. Otherwise I was subject to, enchanted by, and totally absorbed by my new "social" training—for a while.

In my late thirties, sinking into depression, my ideal and ideally competent self collapsed into worthlessness. "Look what you've all done to me" was a whisper I could barely pick up I was so ashamed of it. The only gratification was that I had done my duty—to my husband, children, my parents and Alec's, especially my quintessential mother-in-law—and it was all too much for me. Through Swinburne's "Hertha" I became the Earth Goddess, and the poem took me out of my miserable existence. Now I was no longer a depressed and useless reality but a concept of life, a dream of cosmic wisdom and vision and growth. I learned the forty verses and flowed them out at need.

But thereafter, when I had found my profession, I never did fantasize about it. Case by case, I set my sights on what could be achieved by my clients and on how I could help them achieve it. Case by case I learned, and gained competence and confidence, building a solid structure with plenty of mortar for my bricks. The fantasies I now had were about the far future and a final peace of mind in honorable achievement. I came upon Henley's poem "Margaritae Sorori," learned that one too by heart, and for decades used it almost as a prayer.

My final ideal of myself was all there: the sense of duty, work and wages, final peace, serene and glorious ending.

Death, yes, the final resolution in a perfect amen; but I didn't yet think about what sort of old woman to be. Most women don't until the menopause signals to them. That can be a time of liberation and of choice. For me, active, well, and strong, it brought a great singing of change. Analysis and professional happiness and success had given me status and loosened my bondage. It seemed to me that I had the freedom to make my choice and the capacity to make it come true.

Archetypes that came to mind, the roles old women play, were based on a pattern that was plainly archaic, a time when few survived to old age. I looked at them—the scold, the shrew, the drone, the invalid, the rejected, the female of hate, the inane and the insane, the poisonous witch, the tender nurturant one, and the wise woman—all but one were prototypes of younger or older women I had seen at one time or another in my life or work and I knew that within me I carried the seeds of any or all of those, except that one: had I ever known or known of a truly wise woman, wise in an almost allegorical or mythical sense? I couldn't even picture her but I wanted so to be a wise woman then, and later, and still later!

My family's tradition was matriarchal and tribal, perpetuated by generations of mothers and daughters: keepers of the household gods, founts of wisdom, wellsprings of power. And they tried to be wise, and usually thought that they were, and often were very wise. But not in my sense of wisdom. I had observed selfishness and self-indulgence, materialism, and willfulness, intolerance, and sometimes, rarely, cruelty in these magnificent women.

When did I first learn of old age and what did I learn? I believe I was seven. In childhood on the long walk home from our little country school, I sometimes saw, standing in the doorway of a farmhouse, an old woman. Her gray hair was in wisps, her long apron dirty, and she looked vaguely into the distance. Her head jerked constantly as if it were being pulled by strings. One day she pointed her finger right at me. A witch! I was terrified.

"Who's she?" I asked my brother who knew everything.

"She's nuts, crazy, bughouse. From the lunatic asylum."

The lunatic asylum was the complex of large brick buildings on the other side of our village. Still frightened inside, I pressed my mother for details. "The State Infirmary," she said. That sounded better. "The State Infirmary places out the harmless old people. They help with farm housework. They're better off not shut up all the time." But my fear lingered on and on, of what old age could mean, at its most dire—you become a waste, a reject, and crazy.

A few years later, I was thirteen and taking the train alone to the city, presumably to be met there. Behind me I heard a disturbance, and I turned to see. A strong-armed, strong-faced heavy woman with a hard look pushed ahead of her a little old one. They sat diagonally back of me—the strong one on the aisle seat. The train began to move. The little wizened one cried out, *"J'ai peur! J'ai peur, j'ai peur!"* It was the insane asylum again and my anxiety rose. Now the wizened one was making a scene and screaming out her fear. She tried to climb over the bulk of the body beside her. The strong voice shouted angrily, "No one's going to hurt you. Now keep *quiet!*" But neither one understood the other and the frantic old Frenchwoman only increased her noise.

I'd had one year of French. I wanted desperately to tell the poor thing not to be afraid. But I was terrified of the flood of words that might come out of that twitching, frantic body, words far too fast for me to understand. I couldn't reassure her, not knowing what the problem was or whether she was right to be afraid. And I cringed inside from the mean look on the big one's face. "I don't dare, I'm afraid myself," I thought and I turned and pressed my head against the window pane all the way to the city, trying not to hear what now had become sobs. I didn't know the word then, but I knew it now—total impotence, the impotence of the old and helpless. I grieved over that cowardice of mine for years. (Did it play a part in my later decision to become a psychiatric social worker?)

Rejection, impotence: I understood them better now, curled restlessly on the tousled bed I couldn't bend to smooth out and was too tired to leave for long, than I did in the fantasies of my fifties. Treading the tiny patterns of my days, dreading surprise, taking comfort in habit and repetition, I thought of my father's mother. I was named for my paternal grandmother, and our birthdays were the same day, and for years we celebrated them together in Newport. One morning she said, "You may help me with the dishes today, little Harriet." She was widowed at twenty-eight, and still wore black except on very hot summer days, when she had on her soft gray dress. She was tiny and had a false front to her hairdo which didn't match the gray in the back. (I walked into her bedroom one morning and saw her pinning it on.) Her skirts were very full and to the ground, the belt tight and trim over her corset, her shirtwaist neck-high, the sleeves to the wrist. No one ever saw anything but her face and hands.

I followed her into the pantry wondering why she washed dishes when there were two to help in the kitchen. The sun shone in the pantry windows above the sink, which glowed copper. On the towel rack were three freshly ironed linen dish towels. A low stool-step had been placed before the sink.

Grandmother put on a fresh, large bibbed apron and stepped up. She unbuttoned and turned up her cuffs; she filled the sink with steaming hot water and then vigorously shook the wire soap-shaker until the water bubbled and frothed. First the glasses (to be rinsed later), then silver, cups and saucers, and the breakfast plates. So neat, so orderly, and I tried to make each motion as precise as hers. It was hard.

A soft humming came from her throat as she stood there in the sunlight. It was like a kitten's. She turned and smiled at me suddenly. I saw that she loved to do this unnecessary morning work, and I think I dimly understood even then that the little ritual gave meaning to her days. From her I learned that sometime, when I was old, I too could enjoy little rituals and orderly ways. I did not then see how limited and Victorian she was. Her daughter, Aunt May, ever unmarried, had a fund of fairy stories (they would curl a psychiatrist's hair—they were so full of sexual symbols), and we children would sit by the hour listening, loving the suggestive ones best, but not knowing why. Aunt May had never borne any real responsibility except teaching Sunday school. There is a story about her in the family. Grandmother, then an active seventy-five, went into a large department store and asked a clerk for a dress for a young girl (her daughter). Nothing she was shown suited her. Finally the salesgirl asked, "How old is the girl?" My grandmother thought a moment. "Fifty-two," she said. The matter was soon resolved in another department.

After her mother's death at ninety-two, this same Auntie May developed chest pains. The local doctor suggested her problem was "possibly angina." And so, until her death twenty years later, my aunt stayed in bed, waited on by nurses and eating up her inheritance. My father-in-law, a heart specialist, traveled to see her with his portable electrocardiograph machine and reported that her heart pain was "functional" (no discernible physical cause). My aunt was furious that he had not made a diagnosis that gave her the right to withdraw from life. But what can a specialist do? There was no way that sixty-five years of being infantilized by her mother could now be dealt with. She had chosen her path and was content with it as the least of evils.

I was strong and well when Aunt May took to her bed, and I shared my family's feeling of pitying superiority even as I understood her fears. My tribe spoke of invalids with a faint scorn that suggested, "They don't try. They've got no guts," or the half-bewildered, "What the hell's the matter with her anyhow?"

Curiously, no one ever took that attitude toward my mother, though she was always tired and suffered from neuralgia. She was loved for her patient sweetness and cherished for her difference. Her voice, however, carried no authority in the family councils. But I, growing up in her image, always felt inferior. Warped back, buck teeth, depression, lack of appetite, no energy—my childhood weaknesses kept a kind of constant blush of shame on my mind.

And here it was again, with me on my bed, deeply uncomfortable with my invalid status, unable to ask openly for assistance in anything. "What the hell's the matter with me?" was so often on my mind. One bad bitter day, I was so preoccupied with pain in body and mind that I did not hear the door chime. The front door was wide open to the sunlight and a familiar friend walked in, spoke, heard no answer, worried, came to my bedroom, and entered. I returned from far away, saw her standing there, and half shrieked at her, "Get out!" I scared myself, but I scared her more by this utterly uncharacteristic behavior. She went home and called my son in his office. But he understood. That night he telephoned and asked, "How's everything?" And I replied, "Been busy, writing and thinking," and that was that. He knew enough to leave me alone to sweat this one out.

How horrified my mother would have been; I can hear her solemn voice, "Are you living up to your standards?" This was the closest she came to reproof, once I was grown, and an infallible way of quenching me. But still, for me to have yelled out loud!

My mother's fiber had weakened in her own old age; she had not been able to live up to *her* standards, set once and for all by *her* powerful mother, whose thrall she never escaped, whose example she could not equal. After she was widowed, her interest waned in anything but her family, and after innumerable little strokes we saw her wilting before our eyes. With the return of repressed feeling and memory that can come with aging when guards are down, and of course with accumulating brain damage, Mother's long-strangled anger appeared at last. I could sometimes hear it when I came up the stairs to visit her. It hurt. So I would call out and at my voice her rage turned off like a tap and the calm benignant face turned to me with full recognition as I entered. The effort must have been terrific. She might be paranoid with the nurses and the housekeeper, and accuse them of unmentionable sins, but never at or in the presence of her children. In this area alone, Mother kept her mastery; but everywhere else she was letting go, and we watched, helpless, as, very slowly, her mind flickered out.

Her mother had lived longer, to ninety-two, and kept all her power to the very end, queen of her tribe and something of a sorceress too, absolutely certain of her control and her judgment.

This grandmother was a great lady in her unaffected dignity, unspoken pride, and a mild grace that hid the powerhouse beneath. It's fascinating how certain family stories make an indelible mental impact: mother told me that when young, grandmother was a famous belle (does that scrapbook, still extant, containing accounts of her presence, hair, and clothes at so many Washington parties, suggest a certain vanity?). Her bedroom, wherever she was, contained many long mirrors. But after six children, at the age of thirty-five, she abruptly had all glass removed, keeping, for the rest of her long, long life, only a small one to peer into while fixing her hair. What had *she* seen in the mirror?

No more society after that. She devoted herself to her early-retired husband and her children. She enchanted them with her whimsy and her stories, and in the process lured them into an almost supine adoration. I often wondered how much there was of subtle fear in the ties of the four daughters to her. I never saw her raging or implacable or vituperative, but one sensed such great force, self-discipline, and determination I wouldn't put anything past her.

She was eighty-seven when grandfather died at ninety-eight. I could detect no repining, no change in habits. She continued to keep hands and mind busy with her many quiet interests, never called in a doctor, and never took to bed with any ailment whatever until a few days before her death. And she planned, how she planned, for the future of her tribe, by then fifty-seven living descendants. The charm that flowed out to her children was never bestowed on my generation. There was always candy for us on her table, and cookies in the kitchen, a hammock on her porch, but she never shared thoughts or memories, or the flickering play of mood and imagination. When a new great-grandchild was laid in her lap her look was unfathomable and she studied it with grave wonderment and reverence and was in no hurry to have it removed.

As I grew older I developed mixed feelings about her, sensing a little of the black widow spider. Perhaps I was jealous at Mother's saving her own fun and fancy for the old lady, not for her children, for she visited Grandmother once or twice a day when she was near, and followed her spring, summer, and winter to her three different places of residence. Was Mother afraid of her? She adored her; she couldn't keep away. And where were the men in this matriarchy? They were tenderly cared for, most of their needs were met lovingly, but they remained second-class citizens.

Then there was Mrs. Robey with her cold control. Where did she stand as role model in my imaginary tribe? She was not so much woman as self-appointed stone idol, emblem of ritual. Her dicta were sacrosanct. (When she was informed at the hospital that our second son had already arrived, en route, in the front seat of our car, her sole comment was an anguished cry, *"It isn't done!"* Disillusionment had long since set in and that remark was cherished by me.) I often marveled that Alec had been able to escape any class-consciousness or snobbery.

Handsome, correct to a fault, and diligent in good works, she conducted her life with impeccable self-discipline. In old age, just when comfort *is* so comforting, she lived in rigid parsimony on dwindling capital, in order to maintain her big town house with all its empty bedrooms. We urged an apartment, but apartments, she said firmly, were not done. I felt truly sorry for her in her denial of change, and I came to admire her vigilant, silent, unyielding self-control.

I only once saw it crack. As a Christmas present, we had bought her as good a fur coat as we could afford, and had done up a huge box with our little daughter inside. The three boys carried it in, Christmas Day, and laid it down before the beautifully white-haired erect old lady; then our daughter burst out of the container with the furrier's box in her arms. And Mrs. Robey broke down in tears. Just that once!

Of all the strong controlling respected old women I knew Isabelle Robey was the least like my mother, whose emotions were so close to awareness they wore her out. The two women kept their respectful distances from each other in some instinctive avoidance. To Mrs. Robey's "Look your best to others, that's all that matters," my mother's philosophy countered, "Act well despite how you may feel." And yet, hadn't they something in common, something that was still hampering me? A blindness to so much of their own humanity, a denial that, living on in me, put some ultimate honesty out of my reach?

Of all the roles I could imagine for an old woman, even beyond my mother's wonderful nurturance and her tender cherishing, I had dreamed to grow into the wise woman, the one turned to for her almost vestal calm, for her right answers, for nature lore, and for deep, almost mystic, understanding; the one to whom nothing human is strange or fearful; the one who, in a way, stood for the conscience of the tribe and for its betterment.

By my sixties I no longer idealized any of my relatives, and as I had grown older I had moved beyond their family-preoccupied traditional roles. Training had taught me to think more in terms of the collective good, even as a wise woman does, and to look forward rather than back.

One day a gloomy friend told me in mournful tones that she had recently seen my childhood home, sold to a developer after my mother's death. "Don't ever go back!" she told me. "It will break your heart to see it so horribly changed."

That made me angry. So I went back at once, curious, for one thing, to find out what a broken heart might be like. The rambling house did look small and faceless and nonvital. The old red barn was still there. But what stunned me was the colony of tiny houses that had been built where the country road ran along three sides of our old property. My mother, when she had moved there in 1906, had planted blue spruce and maple trees alternately perhaps every hundred feet, near the stone wall that bordered the land. Now every tree was a great and perfect giant. And below or beside each one, protected and shaded, was a small home, its picture window draped with white curtains, a lamp in the center. There were vegetable gardens on most of these small plots, and children were running about. My mother would never know, but I could rejoice for her. The protective shade, that shade she had created, the country living she had deliberately given to us, were now going to so many families who wanted the same things for their children. And these children must play in the brook that we played in. Only, of course, they would not know how to make little wooden water wheels or find frog-jelly as I had. (Or would they?) And the shy, sky-blue closed gentians would be gone.

Now indeed I saw how my profession had changed me. When we first moved out to that area it was a simple farming community with a green, a flagpole, a trolley, a store, a church, a four-room school, and a piano teacher who struck your knuckles with a ruler if you hit the wrong note. (I didn't last long, and not merely because I had a headache every time just before going.) So we were the only gentry there on the hillside above the town, and the children were "village children," who thought and knew and sometimes said terrible words, and wrote them on the schoolhouse walls and in the smelly basement toilets, but when I brought home two dirty ditties and sang them with glee to Mother, I was permanently silenced on anything scatological.

The knowledge of class differences rose insidiously in me, as bit by bit it was borne in on us: they were the working people, we the gentry, even if we didn't look rich but saved everything for college educations. Certainly we stood aloof. Each of my brothers had a friend from farms nearby, usually for such things as pigpen rat shooting, or some other fine boys' activities. I had no friends there, nor had my parents. *Their* friends came out from town. Only a minister—a woman—became close to Mother, and had tea at our house, but before long she moved to another parish.

So I looked down at the children in school, their occasional lice, their nose-picking, their bad English, their sticking out their tongues at me, their making fun of my clothes. And I too stood aloof, mostly, alone in the school yard observing, with superiority as a defense. At twelve I moved on to be a day pupil in a girls' boarding school and was separated from those "village children" forever. Besides, I had caught diphtheria from them. Alas, at the new school, which I attended only from nine to one, roles were reversed. By the boarders I was looked upon as a "hick" from the country. Again, no friends.

So I learned much too early that precarious and imaginary line between who was accepted and who wasn't, and what "upper crust" was. Then with marriage came further distancing, greater superiority, deeper sense of the privileged few; and the arcane and closely held lore about what was done, what wasn't. But just as my body could never well tolerate a girdle, bra, or even stockings—anything tight or strait-laced or that drew at me—so after two years of indoctrination into everything the city and the Robeys had to offer culturally, including duplicate bridge, a revulsion rose in me and soon I had little left of that sort of snobbery. I didn't need analysis or social work to see through its absurdities, only a sense of humor, and perhaps my growing, late-blooming identification with Alec, who had remained, *mirabile dictu,* free of taint. He was like his father in that.

So much of my secret life, throughout the years, had been played on a stage, a stage of fantasy—I standing alone on the great proscenium, in the floodlights of my imagination, hearing the final tremendous applause. And now, old, I had to step behind the curtains as they drew closed with their little swing and swish, and there I must encounter, face to face, myself; we two alone who never yet did meet—the lonely child who lives on her fantasies because the real thing, the real self, wasn't good enough, and the mature old woman so caught in some past blinding passion that she could see only her own shadow of insubstance.

The wise woman, vestally calm. What a joke now! Only the worthless invalid lying there in bed.

It was but a day or two before I went back to that rolling poem "Hertha," which had so strengthened me when I was desperate forty years before. I had never forgotten any of it and parts of it, unbidden, cried on my tongue now and then. Why should I be ashamed of a searching for concepts of something greater than myself to help me out in the work I had before me—the deepest and highest ideals I could find. Isn't this the stretch of the animal called hominid? My body may have betrayed me but I still had a mind and a soul. And so again I rolled off my tongue the weaving, waving rhythms of nature's song. I quote two widely separated stanzas:

Though sore be my burden
And more than ye know,
And my growth have no guerdon
But only to grow,
Yet I fail not of growing for lightnings above me or death worms below . . .
For truth only is living,
Truth only is whole,
And the love of his giving
Man's polestar and pole;
Man, pulse of my centre, and fruit of my body, and seed of my soul.

CHAPTER 9

"Seek wisdom?" I had two things I'd never had before—time and freedom—so far as there is freedom in ever-present pain.

Having plunged into intense self-awareness and retrospect, I began making notes on old age. A sense of purpose grew in me. My reading was no longer for escape. I was studying.

I tried first to look at the old en masse, objectively. There are so many of us now, the elderly, that we are no longer venerated unless we have achieved greatly. I must learn to think, not of remarkable individuals, but of a class.

The fastest growing segment of the population in this country is that of women sixty-five and over. In 1977 there were 13.9 million of us, compared with 9.6 million men of that age group. And of those over seventy-five, 70 percent were widows. It has been projected by the HEW (Department of Health, Education and Welfare) that by the year 2036 there will be 33.4 million elderly women, compared to 22.4 million men.

The old are poorer, physically and mentally more fragile, and under more stress, than the rest of the population. They are lonelier, but not so lonely as the many horror stories would have one believe. And I was reading everything I could find. These books ranged from concern with the social or political issues to the psychiatric and psychoanalytic (which I hastily eschewed), the religious and the mystic; there were poignant books on nursing homes and various plights of the elderly, the poor and the lonely. There were how-to-prepare-yourself books starting at early middle age, some excellent, but too late for me. And nearly all were written by people much younger than sixty-five. Through my reading I learned clearly that I was now a nonperson in our society.

How are the old looked upon, en masse, by others? We are a burden eating up the Social Security savings of younger workers. We have become slow-witted, handicapped, arthritic, deaf, or blind, unable to use our own judgment or manage our own affairs. And having ceased to be eager, curious, or interesting, having become nonconstructive and noncontributing (we are taking money out of others' pockets if we hold onto jobs), we are poor old things, full of fears, easily rattled, helpless, often needy, difficult, demanding, of no value until we die and, in general, we are a nuisance.

There are, it seems, too many of us. There are so many of us that our paternalistic, kindly, ponderous, bumbling, often constipated federal government—and society in general—is now attempting to study, analyze, and provide for our physical and psychological needs. Mass solutions must be found for the mass problem that we constitute. Mass feeding, mass doctoring, mass housing, and, for the worst nuisances, mass custody. And it's not easy. There are so many of us that exploitation is commonplace. There are so many of us on Medicare and Medicaid that abuses or substandard conditions exist yet pass unheeded in many "lifetime rest homes" or other residences for the aged. Communities do better in creating facilities for comfort such as Meals on Wheels, old-age recreation centers, and so forth. Local volunteers do yeoman work as trustees, visiting committees, and watchdogs: tasting the food, checking the balance sheet, fixing the flowers, or even teaching us to play Bingo. With all their hearts, they want the aged to be happy, mentally alert, and in reasonable health (barring physical handicaps), to be sufficiently fed and adequately warm. All that the aged need do in return is to be very thankful for what they get and grateful to be alive.

Often they—we—aren't. I didn't need books to tell me that. We can be infuriating. What about those individuals who regress to childishness? To a greater or lesser extent they turn their intuition, their sixth sense, into omnipresent suspicion: they fear and mistrust anything new. They are totally self-centered and have no concern for others' feelings. They can be impatient, irresponsible, demanding, ugly, retaliative, dirty and unkempt, spilling and soiling—just like stubborn yet very dependent children. Their memories of the past or stories about themselves tend to be as endless and endlessly repetitive as their self-importance. Their judgment on certain things is as impaired as is their self-control. They may explode in rage or tears at family, friends, or anything that is baffling. They may react to kindness with anger—and to anger with infantile terror.

Research indicates that the more intense a personality change is, the greater the early childhood insecurity must have been. We see some of the greatest oddities in old age in the areas of money and food, since money so frequently comes to represent love given, or love received, or love denied and food has similar connotations. There are those who intensify accumulation and disorder until there is more and more of less and less. One can die alone of starvation or cold, in a house jammed to the roof with newspapers, magazines, cartons, containers, and money stashed in odd places—plenty of money—and one can die impoverished in every way, still starved for things that represent, crazily, the love one did not get. (The media can get quite gleeful over such tragedies.)

A man who has tended toward frugality all his life, even amid plenty, may suddenly become wildly profligate in money matters. Alternatively, a woman who has always been a generous spender becomes tight in face and stingy in spending until she is utterly miserly, amassing not only money but everything else, and scrimping on those close to her as she scrimps on herself. There is the old woman who stashed away bits of food in her closet, remaining indifferent to the smell, the mold and rot that resulted, yet she may have been brought up as a "lovely lady." There is the man who has always been rigorously polite and controlled, if not overpunctilious, who now changes into someone the family is ashamed to have in sight: dirty, slovenly, spilling food—yet somehow still able to keep a close rein on his financial affairs.

Every little child feels for a while that he is omnipotent, and a great blow to that sense of power occurs when at two or three years he has to knuckle under to the greater power of a parent: "Be toilet trained, or else!" Now, in old age, having been obedient to that training—by habit or by fear—all his life, he dares at last to break through and say once more, "I'm the king of the castle!" He doesn't care what others think and he squanders or hoards at will.

One appraiser, in going through the estate of a deceased old man, finally came to the bathroom. Leading off it was a large closet filled with dozens of medicine bottles, some empty, some half filled, many dated years before. The appraiser's first impulse was to throw them all out as valueless. But then he had a hunch. He opened each bottle and emptied it. Mixed in with pills were quantities of unset precious and semi-precious gems. What a dreadful symbol of an old man's fear and needs!

Abstemiousness and frugality are one thing; avarice is another. Excessive greed and secrecy and meanness and intolerance are especially hard for the average person to sympathize with. Almost equally exasperating can be the childish elderly person who is dependent, complains constantly, and gets choleric at any positive suggestion of help. At another extreme there are those who become obscene in thought and words, or who, formerly stiffly rigid about sex, now pinch the bottoms of females and snicker as they do so.

The attendants in nursing homes or institutions for the elderly have to deal with every variety of personality oddity or disorder, from fantastic cleanliness to filth, from rage and violence to helpless timidity, from constant demands to apathy. How can they stay calm and kind day after day? Or do they? Is it the patient, loving, cheerful ones who sustain them?

For those who have never paid their way in life there is a sense of lack of fulfillment that seems to me to be particularly conducive to childishness in old age. There are those who have lived on unearned income or inherited money, those who got by on others' shoulders, those whose jobs were totally unsatisfying. They come toward the end of life with no sense of integrity, no feeling of having feet solidly on the ground, no sense of satisfaction at having done a good day's work for a good day's pay. We all know the very wealthy women who feel so entitled that nothing will ever suit them, and their complaints encompass everything.

Or there is the pitiable situation of some of the elderly poor who have earned and saved and should be secure in old age; who have worked in pride and dignity and paid their way and who now find that their high principles and their steadiness have left them impoverished and bereft. They are tragic figures. Their eyes are downcast as they ask for help. A few will not ask.

Only the psychiatrically oriented in our communities are coming to grips with the real hunger in us, a hunger that is far more important than the millions spent on ramps in every city and public building, essential though these may be. For the pride of the old is vulnerable and always at hazard.

We have a hunger for respect and consideration, for autonomy, the right to decent physical and medical care if we become dependent upon government, for the right to a little dignity and a little privacy, and respect for our own integrity, for the right to let our minds and our bodies tell us when it is time to die, and not be subjected to superfluous and often demeaning medical treatment and experiments in the name of science and Aesculapius; and even for the right to be called Mr. or Mrs. if that enables us to retain the fading sense of self-respect a little longer. We old want not to crawl.

So many of us—56 million voters projected by 2036—what a mighty bloc, would we but all vote and use our accumulated wisdom when so doing! I read about lobbying groups and activist groups (like the Gray Panthers) and belatedly joined the A.A.R.P. (American Association of Retired Persons) and high time, for I soon found out all the benefits I had missed. I have always cast my ballot, but to speak up and out myself, even were I physically energetic, was so alien to my nature and to my type of mind, which could not grasp statistics or graphs or totalities or bodies of knowledge such as geriatrics, or broad issues in depth, and as I could be argued down by anyone, I, like Mother, never raised my voice. In the old days I always did my share in the door-to-door solicitations for such causes as the Community Fund and the Heart Fund drives, but was apt to end up saying, after hearing a hard-luck story, "Just don't give anything this year." My putty quality of nonaggression, nonopposition (one simply keeps adverse opinions to oneself) made the thought of speaking out publicly for any cause anathema to me, even though I watched with admiration my mother's sisters, in the forefront of parades, shouting for women's suffrage, birth control, and other strongly believed in rights. I shuddered at their courage and would never, never try to argue with them on any subject. In this area I *was* afraid, afraid of any loud or angry voice.

When I had read what the many books had to say, and found little nourishment in most of them, since none evoked the actual feelings the old were experiencing, and since I could not find what I craved—a first-person exploration of the dark continent of age by a traveler who knew the language, then I would write my own book, darn it. I would express and share what I was now becoming aware of about myself. Maybe others had the same need as I. And that would have to be my contribution. I would not try to map my new continent, only to understand and faithfully record what I found. I would not speak for the many contented old. They might travel with me as tourists if they would. I *could* not speak the feelings of all the old who suffer, who are hungry or cold, alone, deprived, or friendless; for those in despair; for the battered and the maimed and the hopeless; for those who have turned against or been turned against by their offspring; for the derelicts and the criminals; for those in nursing homes with callous caretakers; for those who are frightened and timid, shrinking from any act that might betray their existence; for all in anguish who have found no religion to sustain them; for those who are wealthy and demand pampering, but live in terrible loneliness and anger within because any love that comes to them seems to come in hope of gain; for the very old who have lost all that belong to them, including friends, and for whom and to whom no person comes with love; for all who see nothing ahead and are terrified of death as a great swallowing horror in a nightmare; for those who have no curiosity, particularly those who are aware enough to know that they have failed to fulfill themselves and their potential. I did and do not feel so much pity for those for whom senility has been the result of brain damage or the only answer to the inertia of deep depression. They no longer are concerned with the future and have no perspective on their plight, having lost or let fade the anxieties of self-awareness and the ache of responsibility and guilt.

I could empathize with and grieve for them, but I could speak only of that which I knew firsthand, I who have adequate financial resources, who live alone enjoying solitude, with many descendants who come to me because they want to come. I, with all the consolations of all but bodily comfort, set forth into my unexplored continent. But what I was to find at the heart of darkness was less a consolation than an eerie challenge.

CHAPTER 10

My descendants visited me because they wanted to come, I said. Was it from love? Concern? Duty? For fun? And I thought about us as parents and the amazing variety of personalities that come out of our (and others') training. Should we carry guilt over idiosyncrasies in our offspring that trouble us?

I remember our firstborn and his tulip. He was about three years old when he wandered into forbidden territory, the garden of a neighbor who raised famous prize tulips, where every blossom was sacrosanct. He came home clutching an enormous blood-red one and I cried out, "Oh, no!" But he held it up to me, and his eyes were shining, so I said it was beautiful and then I began the parental process. I tore one petal off after another—"These are the petals, see?" Then I showed him the stamen and the sepal, the leaves and the stem, pulling all apart. "Now, you know how a flower is made." He cried hard, ran to his room, and wouldn't come out for a long time. I did not yet know what I had done, but guilt was with me. It was years before I realized how I had robbed him.

I think of the time when I visited the second grade class of one of my children. I sat in the back of the room that November morning, and suddenly the first snow of the year began to fall, the flakes huge, almost plum-sized. "Snow," someone whispered. Every face turned to the windows that ran the length of the wall. There was no sound whatever. The children were utterly rapt, their very breathing low and still, caught in some magical primitive thinking. The teacher did not speak. She gave them one minute. Two. The air outside was white and thick and luminous. Then one child yelled, "Snow!" and all hell broke loose. "All right," said the teacher firmly, "now let's get back to work. Now let's see. Who was reading?" "But *why* is snow?" asked a little boy. "Not *why* is snow, *what* is snow?" Miss Norris said. No one answered. She began, "Water freezes at thirty-two degrees

Fahrenheit in moisture-laden air. . . ." I left. Poor Miss Norris!

At college I majored in premedical courses, passed the chemistry only after several tries, and came to graduation with minimum marks and the memory of a psychological test from which it was clear that my retention of facts and figures was abysmally low (almost zero), but that my scores in those areas which challenged ingenuity, adaptability, quick perception, and intuition were extremely high. My four-year battle with the data of science had been too draining. I gave up all thought of medicine, but I took home, along with the rotten-egg smell of the chem lab, and the formaldehyde stink of biology, my precious dissecting kit, symbol of a lost dream.

The following fall, at home, idle, fast falling in love for the first time in my life, done with studying forever, I hoped, I enrolled in a class in drawing at the Fogg Museum. Since I came from an artistic family, maybe this could be my forte. The first object for our pristine paper, one plain dull straight chair. I could *not* draw it. It was as much a stick figure as any man or woman I would draw today. The instructor gave me up. Marriage and motherhood had to be my métier and my life.

The time came when three young sons, one dead squirrel, and the dissecting kit met; I went to work and exhibited what, inside us, we had in common with all animals, and told of our beginning out of the primordial soup, our climb up from the sea, and of the eternal salt in us. I feel now as if I crooned as I talked. For a few months all small animals—a cat struck by a car, a shot woodchuck, a duck—fell to my scalpel. But the best was a mouse in a trap. Three pink curled pea-sized babies within a placenta. A decent burial followed all our dissections. Two sons became doctors. The oldest had been already too well indoctrinated by us, such ignorant young parents.

We try so hard to be sensitive. We try so hard to be good. And fair, and honest, and dutiful. And our children try in return. But nothing is simple.

Deeply I pity the childless old. There are, among them, the unmarried women who have never known a man; those who yearned but could never conceive; those who chose not to conceive; those whose child or children died prematurely; those whose relationship with an only offspring became so bitter that all contact was irrevocably broken. I sense a deep secret sorrow, an emptiness in these women for whom no one exists of their own flesh to whom to entrust the possessions, beliefs, knowledge, and memories of a lifetime.

But perhaps it is simpler for them. The reverberating emotions that flow between different generations (or between members of the same) are universal, and when these reverberations become thunderous they give us, out of the innate terror-cry of man-out-of-control, many of the Bible stories, the great sagas and epics, the Greek tragedies, the passions in all our criminals, the seeds of our own love and hate, all incest and murder, reverence and awe at their highest; and in the last analysis man-against-himself, whose parents are internalized in him as conscience. In our day the police blotter tells the stories, and though the stories are tragic they are rarely heroic.

Children of aging parents who are on the path to death wish the old ones might put no financial, physical, or emotional burdens on them. They want them to die peacefully without pain, full of love and tenderness and pride in their offspring.

Parents want the children to present a

face of success and fulfillment and love, as if to say, "Behold us, your descendants. We are happy and well and have no problems, thanks to you, and we love you dearly." Elderly parents also wish that their children would give any help and support that might be needed, and give it freely—without being asked.

Alas, that it might be so! But it would be dull as hell for them. And the opposite state of affairs is equally simplistic in the father's "How sharper than a serpent's tooth it is to have a thankless child," or his moan, "Absalom, my son Absalom—Would God I had died for thee!" Or for the child to respond, "I didn't *ask* to be born, did I? It's all your fault."

From picayune and petty to epic in its intensity, the battle between close kin goes on, and every adjective applies at one time or another.

Were I of the animal kingdom I would fight to the death to keep safe my cubs or pups to the stage when they could fend for themselves. Then I would snap at them if they tried to suckle. Their training over, I would know them no more as I waited for instinct to tell me when to mate again. But it is very hard for a human mother to kick a child cleanly out of the nest even though her husband insists it is time. It was hard for me to say no when our young went through that period of enjoying their own independent lives yet wanting home too, and good meals without warning, and all the other benefits of being a loved and sometimes indulged child. But if they had left us prematurely or in rejection, I'd have been hurt. I still have an incredible letter to Alec from his broken-hearted mother, written in an early year of our marriage, disowning him emotionally and financially for giving up everything she had spent years inculcating in him: weekly church, settlement work, practicing his music, pursuit of the arts, no alcohol, and utter obeisance to parents. Of course I was the culprit. For without being told how, Alec had swiftly found his own sweet delights. Mrs. Robey was of the school that believed an only son, married or not, should contact his mother every day—by visit, letter or telephone. Some never completely relinquish an only son to another woman. Resentments slowly grew in me, though in my innocence I didn't recognize them as such at first. I felt that Alec's tie to his mother was a beautiful thing and that I must foster it.

A crisis came over naming my only daughter, her only granddaughter. When I gave the baby my own good, plain, five-generations-old "Harriet Lyman" instead of my mother-in-law's "Isabelle," it was the first time I had ever insisted on my own will and stood on my own two feet. Mrs. Robey ostracized me for a year, but she came around finally and accorded me a new respect.

I owe her a valuable lesson—that we should never, never hold our children (or mates) in a cage of our control. Her methods—and the consequences to Alec—wrote the moral in black and white. How much more subtle, because unconscious, was the cage in which my tender mother enclosed me: her values were built into me, under my skin.

Mrs. Robey's second lesson to me was more generous. A couple of months before she died, at eighty-four, she said abruptly to me, "I was very cruel to you when you were first married. I'm sorry!" Then she changed the subject so fast there was no chance for me to even say, "Thank you." To have known all those years; so accurately to use the word *cruel;* and to be able to get an apology out—was this also the first, ever? I loved and admired her for that.

For us of the oldest generation, it seems to me that before we die it is important that we lose face—since we have so little face to lose—and make peace with close relatives and children no matter how bitter have been earlier deeds, words, or thoughts. It has taken two to make the quarrel that bred the hurt and anger. The elderly alone can say the words that bring relief, and all are the richer, including the other members of younger generations who observe a change from a distance.

In clans like ours, at least, one knows one's presence will matter for generations. Without that final honesty of Mrs. Robey, I could probably not have helped Alec and the children honor her memory. I could never do as my mother's mother did when, editing the family correspondence, she destroyed letters that showed the authors in an unfavorable light. But only by knowing both the good and the bad and the battle between, can our ancestors become truly human to us.

Denial takes another and sadder form in families where a middle-aged child has never made peace with a parent's fallibility, has never given up a need to feel that Mother

(Father) is perfect, which means that they must never be unsupportive or dependent or sick. When that parent begins to fail, so much anxiety is aroused in the aging child that the relationship can become strangely warped, each individual feeling the anger of abandonment. Then no communication is clear-cut, no decisions are comfortably based on reality, and guilt becomes an encompassing but invisible miasma.

Sometimes I end a family telephone conversation with my heart laden, laden. My children are not telling; I'm not knowing; but they're hurting. Which is worse, O my children? Your pretending all is well, but your voices giving the lie; or your drawing me into your pain and making me part of it? Yet if you hide everything I will wilt on the vine, for then I can only shadowbox and feel guilt at the way I brought you up. Better you give me a chance to feel and to share what you feel. That may ease the ache for you in my womb, and some of your burdens may ease too. And perhaps, since I can still know in my bones the manic or depressed agonies of adolescence, I can be a sounding board for the very young as well. We will then all have shared. It is hard to deceive the very old, who, if their minds are clear, read body language and unspoken thoughts as well as the very small child. Moreover, the elderly can guess pretty well what the young are feeling, having felt much the same themselves once. Nor should we be shocked if, for example, a daughter in her late fifties feels bitter: "My husband is like a child, my children and my grandchildren need me, and now my parents are making emotional demands. I can give no more!" We've been there, too. And we too, of course, felt ashamed and did our best to hide it. Only very late do most mothers frankly face and acknowledge emotional depletion: it is not a little thing.

I do not necessarily want to give love all my life, but I have to love because I am human and have been loved. I do not necessarily want to hate, but I have to hate because (as I have learned from experience) hate lies just around the corner from love. I do not want to be tied, in love and hate, to my offspring till the day I die, but I have to, for the womb never forgets. My blood and my children's blood once ran in enclosed circles. My poisons became their poisons and my anxieties theirs. Whenever my children, young or old, hurt emotionally, my womb contracts too.

Yet in old age most passions have quieted, perhaps because our lives are now more bound up in ourselves, perhaps because we no longer have the energy to give full vent to deep emotions. And we have seen and felt so much of drama in a long lifetime that, in retrospect, we know how troubles came and went. We are tired of unnecessary emotion and we take life more philosophically.

I have found it important to remember that if and when a child of any age feels betrayed in some way, and flounces off so angrily that communication is broken, we need only wait in love and patience, showing neither hurt nor retaliation while he goes through his pain. A month? Six months? A year? Two? He'll be back. Meanwhile we can continue calmly with birthday or Christmas messages or gifts. It is almost impossible to maintain the fires of anger year after year when there is absolutely no fuel. We can sweat out our pain for ourselves and our children. Time has given perspective and relief. As we suffered, so will they, and some of us know that a totally painless life is a totally empty life. It's all part of learning and becoming.

There is one great gift a parent may receive. I watch middle-aged sons or daughters deliberately dealing with past hurt or present confusion, going through mental growth and resolving suffering with or without professional help. I am incredibly grateful, for they are doing for themselves what I could not do for them. And at the same time they are confirming to me that I did truly make them the most indispensable gift of all—their freedom to grow on their own.

Conversely, and truly I know this, if a parent gets the courage to change old responses, old stereotypes toward his children (again, with or without professional help), the young observe with wonder and then see their way clear toward further emotional maturation. The air between the generations, no longer befogged, can sparkle.

December of 1978 came after five months almost entirely in or on bed. And with that bleak month arrived the anniversary of Alec's death three years before, and Christmas with its demands seemed utterly meaningless, as did old friends bearing thoughtful little gifts. I was so tired! Tired of pain! Tired of myself! The young wanted the traditional party—it was the one chance for the family to get together, the cousins to exchange news, deepen friendships and loyalties, introduce fresh boy or girl friends. So they brought all food, set up the arrangements, and made me feel loved and pampered, while courteously acting as if nothing were wrong. The granddaughters worked as a team, and their individual gifts to me, since cooking was such an effort for me, were food made by themselves and packed in aluminum containers for my deep freezer, coq au vin, ratatouille, veal scaloppine, quiches (a grandson made one), pies, cranberry, lemon or zucchini breads —wonderful gifts, with each grandchild recollected in the later tranquillity of each bite.

My absent western son sent six tapes all taken from live concerts and all starting or ending with his voice, "Specially recorded for Harriet Robey" with some instructive words on the composer and his works. Always, when I heard his voice, my heart leapt up insanely in extraordinary joy! It was as if I must rush to the hi-fi to get a glimpse of him, some verbal exchange with him, before he disappeared. Or I would sit silent, picturing those words "Recorded Especially For," shining through the lifetime of that often difficult boy, whose love, in our rare visits, flowed so purely.

For my part I gave chiefly checks or new banknotes, and a card to everyone promising a copy, autographed, of the family book I had been writing, which wasn't yet off the press.

Before the month was out, I started to commit to paper the description of Alec's death that begins this book—and suddenly he came back to me. I was not so alone when alone. I hung his picture near my bed where I could constantly glance up at it. Don't ask me why I hadn't done that before.

CHAPTER 11

I expected nothing better of 1979 but I found that there was one great difference. Once I had started writing—first notes, then on a scrawled-over pad, then by dictating machine to a typist, via the mail—the words flowed, and that flow had nothing and everything to do with pain. Often ideas poured out without thought or plan, and I felt a blaze of amazed delight.

I had learned that freedom of flow from the voluminous nonthinking, nonevaluative rush of my pen that had gone on for years in my notebooks when I was in emotional distress and that generally ended with interpretation and some sort of catharsis. "Now I see what I'm up to!" The recent family book, however, was an orderly assemblage and arrangement of historical facts, written with my mind constantly on psychological factors as they appeared through the history of our clan, and with one eye always open to potential family reactions. And then there were some diversions for my own pure creative pleasure.

This book must be different still. After reading one psychoanalytical tome on gerontology and a few articles, I found that the material utterly repelled me, even as it confused me. I no longer could use that familiar orientation. Let the chips fall where they might! I wanted observation and reporting and findings: first, of what it felt like to be old, and miserable to boot, and second, to record what happens and what one thinks about during the aging process. And I wanted, eventually, to gain insight and some forward momentum without having to belabor my reasons for wanting them.

The book grew more and more autobiographical as my work proceeded. I found myself discarding sheaves of observations on the feelings of the elderly in their day-to-day existences. And I found there was a connection between pain and creativity. There were those times when medication didn't seem to help one iota. I swore as I looked at the four-hour wait ahead. Occasionally, I'd force myself to get up and out and walk as hard and as freely as I could. Then I might return with an easier back, but generally I crawled home like a whipped dog. The usual distractions did nothing, family visits and alcohol muted pain briefly, only to intensify it afterward. But when my writing ran freely I got a sense of a flight to freedom, and doors opened in many directions. I became more and more puzzled about pain, for it now seemed almost like a catalytic agent at times. Wasn't it trying to tell me something?

One evening, after a perfectly awful day, I turned on the TV to the start of "Wild, Wild World of Animals." On the screen was a cow in the act of eating grass. There was the cow, head down, jaws chomping rhythmically, there was the green grass, disappearing. Suddenly, as if my conscious brain had taken flight, I was seeing for the first time in my life a cow eating grass. I stared and then, for a second or two of crazy joy, I *was* the cow eating grass.

I breathed, and it was over, I was myself again. What had happened? It felt so pure it was incandescent. Had my small son felt like this as he beheld that tulip, before I spoiled everything?

My unimaginative Alec, who was afraid of feeling, dumbfounded me once. He and I sat at the breakfast table one early April morning, just before we went to work, looking out through the long glass windows of our former home. A very heavy wet snow had fallen overnight, the sun was up, and the huge hemlocks outside were loosening their burden, which fell in soft masses and plops to the ground. One branch after another sprang back into place.

We both started to speak at once, but Alec's words came first. "I could sit here all day falling off the trees." There was an unfathomable look on his face. What I, on the other hand, had been going to say was something like "Isn't it beautiful?" (And here am I, expressing it.) I had wondered at the time, and often since, if I could ever achieve that pure and selfless immediacy of being, that primal freshness.

I'd had hints lately: new perceptions that seemed to brighten awareness as they flickered across it, like butterflies I couldn't catch. When one searches for a word, the exactly right one sometimes appears, a word you never use and didn't know you knew.

But no other word would have done as well. But far bigger than a word, whole new ideas, associations, understandings and memories fluttered into my consciousness; or even paragraphs of descriptions that hardly needed editing.

Searching back, I associated those "butterfly" insights with pain, perhaps because it was some kind of stimulus to abandonment of responsibility. Or could it have to do with the chemistry of the brain? I had read somewhere that joy is the emotion that goes with heightened consciousness and that the state can be stimulated by pain. I had learned from a son and then read further about the beta endorphins and enkephalins, the brain's natural opiates: Lewis Thomas had explained in *The Medusa and the Snail* why a mouse feels no pain as the cat chews it up. Could it be that I was experiencing visionary moments that gave me a fleeting sense of soaring far above run-of-the-mill thinking? In any case, the experience was one of pure butterfly joy.

One day there leapt out at me from a page the recent findings on the left and right hemispheres of the brain. I had, from way back, been aware of and vaguely troubled by a dichotomy in myself. If I had a job that dealt with reality—like houseguests or moving, or Christmas or traveling, I was utterly efficient, holding long lists in my mind, moving smoothly from the demands of one activity to another; logical, sensible, efficient and ingenious about *things,* but I couldn't write a paragraph or have an original thought.

At other times when I was studying or writing or observing nature or letting my mind go free, I was inefficient, remote, forgetful of appointments and unaware of the disordered house. Then I dreaded using the telephone, even if a call was important; but I also felt creative, visionary, and in a kind of seventh heaven. Word-ingenuity flowered. I always felt guilty about this and it made Alec anxious.

My two worlds never fully fused. I saw now that I had been in a constant life battle over this one. In childhood we were supposed to be active during the day—it could be play or reading an approved book when we were young, it could be sports when we were older—but lolling or dreaming or slumping or looking vague were ill tolerated. With analysis both my emotions and my associations broke loose—frighteningly at first. But as I began to run free on all fronts I gained confidence. And now at last—forty years later—I understood what it was all about. Never again need I feel delinquent when I flowed into my other world, when I created in a mist of forgetfulness of reality. And I read that the right hemisphere was an incandescent state of mind and had its own infinity and—in another book—that it has an IQ of 200. Well *that* was a challenge! And further thought suggested to me that this was man's early brain in full and uncensored free touch with all things and all of himself.

Virginia Woolf said in *A Room of One's Own,* "A woman writing thinks through her mother." I didn't want to think through my mother, as if she and I were one and as if my thoughts must pass through hers. Nor did I want to think her through, as if to analyze our relationship even further. She was now twenty years interred in her urn beside Father's in the niches of our forebears and I had settled her happily into oblivion. My memories of her were tender, if sometimes wry, and she seldom came into my mind. When she did it was as a figure of pure mildness, the sweetness of one who had never consciously recognized evil. And yet now I knew I had to look. So I thought *of* her, not *through* her, not yet.

Up to the time of my analysis she had been my idol (to Alec's annoyance), and she could disconcert me horribly by her rare gentle question: "Are you living up to your standards?" I had quite successfully blotted out anything negative about her. But in analysis I wasted a lot of time and money before I could open a crack to the idea that Mother could be anything but perfect. That dike was broached finally after a dream of her destroying me, first by trying to drown me, and next, when I had almost escaped, with a poison bomb. It was only then that memories, so long repressed, could surface, and many of them were colored by a rare rage and fury on her face. The earliest—I was in my crib and she was looking down at me and the distorted look she wore was blinding. What was I doing? I could only, later, guess. Another time: I was allowed to see her shortly after my brother's birth. I was two and a half. I stood at the foot of the bed that had upright bars and I could see her clearly, lying half on her side, the long plait of hair down over her shoulder, and that baby at her breast—*my* breast, *my* milk! (I had been nursed for well over a year.) And I gripped those bars in my hands so hard it hurt and Mother's face grew awful and she said, "Don't you ever look that way again. You must always love your little brother." And later still—some months later probably—I tried to get rid of him for good. What was the heavy thing I crashed down on his head? I don't know. It glanced off. What was the punishment? I don't know. But never will I forget that same look.

I aped her slavishly. Our relationship had been such that where she was unafraid, I must be unafraid, where she was a semi-invalid, I must be one, and was, even as a child. Where she saw sin I must see it, and since sex was bad and evil it should be so for me; where the body must be clean, pure and undefiled, so must be mine; where the mind could hold no evil, no lust nor hate, so must mine be pure as spring water and as innocent of taint.

All my anger at her washed out, once I understood it, as clean as the sands of the beach. What remained was our sense of shared compassion for each other. One little thing only irritated me: to the end of her writing days, her letters were headed 4 A.M.

or 5 A.M. or 6 A.M. In other words, *she* couldn't sleep either. Poor Mother? What a pity, Mother dear! And why tell me about it and make me sad too? I now knew it was her way of saying by not saying, "I'm lonely: I'm sad. I need your love."

As she failed toward the very end I spent the nights near her. One early morning, as I entered her room I was told, "She's going." I sent the nurse down to get coffee and to stay until I called, and I sat by Mother's bed and held her hand and said over and over, "This is Harriet. I love you, Mother. Everything is all right now. I'm your Harriet and I love you." And whether she was dimly aware or not did not matter. I heard and felt her last soft breath go out . . . God bless! . . . I kissed her. I called the nurse.

That night, at home at last, drained after a long day of activity with my siblings and the necessary others, I sat by the fire with Alec and we had our cocktails, and for the first time there came to my mind the fact that no longer would we have to economize, be cautious and so frugal. I mentioned this to Alec.

"Want to know what I'm going to buy tomorrow?"

"What?"

"A new wastebasket for under the kitchen sink."

We both laughed. But that was it. Economy. Frugality, since my childhood. She, who would buy nothing for herself, indulge herself in no way in spite of now being well off financially, had left that taboo also on me in spite of my attempts to break through it.

My thoughts of her brought up one sharp hospital memory. It was about 2 A.M. I'd had another operation but was no longer in pain. I felt only a deep contentment and gratitude for life. My door was wide open, at my request, for tonight I wanted to sense people and the subdued activity of the small hours. My sleeping pill had worn off but I lay at peace, knowing the ability of my body to do its own healing as long as I did not confuse it with crossed fires of emotion.

Around and about I could feel the great hospital breathing quietly. Even the nurses moved more softly. Most offices were closed, most patients asleep; but emergency, X-ray, operating rooms were alert, waiting—waiting. These were far below me. The air conditioner purred softly. Then through sealed windows I heard the distant ambulance cry—louder—louder—until the siren ceased suddenly. There would be swift activity down there now. A shooting? Accident? Heart attack? Someone's life hanging in the balance?

Across the hall from me was the open door of a young woman who had had open-heart surgery a couple of days before. These patients, I knew, had private nurses around the clock, for their lives were precarious. I had been watching them come and go, but from where I lay I could see only the foot of the bed. There had been no sound whatever from that room. Now I watched the nurse leave, probably for a coffee break. The patient must be resting quietly.

Then came the first words, a call. "Mummy." Then, louder and more intense, "Mummy!" And then an anguished loud wail, "Mummy!" that broke off suddenly. I listened a moment. With an instinctive foreboding, I rang my bell, the night nurse came and I pointed, "There may be trouble in there." She hurried out. Another nurse, moving swiftly on soft rubber soles, arrived. They were whispering. The first one came across the hall and without a word closed my door firmly. Then I knew. There followed other faint sounds outside my door. Nothing mattered now; there was work to be done in there. I lay quietly.

Shortly I felt the hospital breathing softly once more, and in sudden deep acceptance of inevitability I slept. For the young woman—God's will be done. And for me? My time will come.

In the morning the nurse woke me and I looked at once across the hall. I could tell from the folded sheets and white cotton spread at the foot of the bed that it was ready and waiting. . . .

As I look back I think of something the first Pope John Paul said. John Paul with his mild childlike face, his sweet smile, his acknowledgment of his unworthiness and unreadiness to pick up a burden so alien to him; trusting and loving as I imagine St. Francis of Assisi to have been. "God is my father," Pope John Paul said; "even more, God is my mother."

Yet there was some confusion still about Mother, something not yet finished. I wanted to stop thinking. I wanted a little time of stillness. I wanted myself to be one great silence like death. Only not death, but an intense aliveness in nothingness. Silence from the clamor of the rat race of my mind. Silence from the emotions that flowed across me, silence from the chattering chiding of the matriarchy that was always watching me. I was afraid of my pain and my life in bed. I was afraid, perhaps, of what that little door to the cow had opened up.

One day I called the Transcendental Meditation Center in the city and a man came out to me. In my ignorance I had visualized the arrival of a swami, flowing hair, beads, huge beard, long saffron robe, and sandaled feet. My poor neighbors! Instead he was a most establishment-looking man with a briefcase. And he was very, very earnest. With a picture of the Maharishi set up before him, he went through some mumbo jumbo that he did not translate. But with him I learned to drift or draw down into quietness and absence of thought and even a sense of loss of body. But when I was alone, and doing my twenty minutes of meditation morning and evening, it became only a time when, undistracted from thought, my back spoke so loudly I could not be still in my acute discomfort. I did, however, continue to mutter my euphonious mantra for a few weeks longer before its effect died on me or I died to it.

In May I instituted another desperate search

for an escape route from my encagement. My son and I visited a noted city consultant. I went with my X-rays, the fresh myelogram, and a timid hope. The new doctor was kind and thorough, and above my head the two doctors talked together. I heard the word *functional* and I gritted my teeth. It had been used too often with me years before when I had a real physical injury.

The doctor turned to me and said, "What should be done is to fuse the vertebrae here, here, and here. Then a body cast for six months. After that I can't guarantee anything. I can do it, but at your age. . . ."

I declined fast.

He then advised another kind of brace. When it eventually arrived, that fine expensive steel-boned contraption held my body so ramrod-straight (in its one absolutely intolerable position) that I was suddenly thrust back into adolescence and all its indignities.

Another hope gone. So I got mad. Mad at specialists, braces, doctors en masse. Mad at medicine and my son. Mad particularly at myself. Of course I'd known there were functional elements, but his saying so put me back in bed with my Aunt May—too old, caught in a past of hopeless unknowns, one of the weak sick sisters. Shame!

Quite inexplicably I called the excellent retirement-cum-nursing home in our area and applied for admission. My startled children were appeased only when I told them there was a long, long wait and that this was insurance for my mind and that I didn't want to be caught, in case of need, in a second-rate one. But I knew there was laughter and tenderness there. My mind was now running strongly in the direction of the road that ends.

How do we prepare for the eventuality of a nursing home—that fateful stepping-stone to death? I was already trying to put my physical and mental house in order. It seemed that by moving into a new simplicity I could prepare both for living and dying.

In fact, I'd been in my sixties when the desire to accumulate possessions first left me. Up to then I had worn a lean, hungry, and envious look when I went into stores. But as the tide slowed, stopped, and turned, I needed to discard and to simplify, to throw or give away everything not used in the last few years, but to save treasures that held real sentiment. I did it the Japanese way—keep some in sight, some hidden, and alternate them lovingly every few months. Treasures like to rest in the dark now and then.

We can prepare by cleaning out files in our desks, by discarding old papers that will have no value or use to descendants, and do the same with everything from attic to cellar. We can label material such as "will," "bank accounts," "marriage certificate," "military papers," "deeds," "mortgages." But documents, letters, and even furnishings that have historical or family significance should be carefully organized and saved, and even designated as to who would inherit what. Grown children can get curious about their forebears, and the juicier and more exciting the anecdotes the more real an ancestor becomes.

Up till now, however, I had kept blinders on when I read about nursing homes, since the stress in the literature was on the poor and the impotent in the Medicare-supported homes that exist for making money out of the unfortunate and forgotten. Thank God, I could afford better. Thank God there were good homes such as the one I had elected, where patients enjoy the companionship of contemporaries and where they are relieved of the burden of feeling they are a burden.

In such homes, as far as possible, the patient's individuality is respected. Each one has the chance to be as content as his personality allows him to be. (There are always those for whom nothing will ever be right.)

But even if you can afford the best, take care! I had read, "If you want to commit murder without guilt send your parents to the most costly nursing home to be found." A friend of mine described one such where she visited a very old blind friend. She told of a cruel, hard-faced, angry nurse, the utter disregard of human feelings, the many open doors off the lushly carpeted corridor, and not one sound from those occupied rooms. Once there were sudden great sobs and a nurse, passing, spoke angrily, "Stop it! You'll upset the other patients!" shut the door and moved on down the hall. Horribly expensive, everything plush, horribly sterile, horribly static, all muted and all for show. No love or caring whatever. Personally, I would rather be in a nursing home where a comfortable, warm-hearted attendant slapped me on the behind and said, "Let's get going, old woman! Sure, you can do it!"

Anyone going into an institution or home must be prepared for losses; of independence, of autonomy, of a certain amount of personal privacy, loss of the old familiar home ways and surroundings, of friends dropping in. Unless you are bedridden, you must take your meals with others, and endure institutional food and a daily regimen such as you have not suffered since childhood.

And for the impoverished, there is too often the prospect of callousness and neglect, lack of cleanliness, inadequate medical care, of devaluation and rudeness at simple human plaints; and fear, fear of anger, of disregard, of sadistic avoidance, of punishment. All without any rights to call your own. And always fear of fire. Do we not, when we hear of many deaths in a nursing home fire, put ourselves in such a predicament for a moment of fear? Bedridden, bewildered, slow to react, and too terrified to cooperate in any way even if we were mobile? And the flames coming nearer!

In the village of my childhood there was not only a Lunatic Asylum, but a Poor Farm for indigent old people who had no relatives. From the road I could see the bent old men working in the vegetable garden or carrying in wood, and the equally old women hanging clothes on the long lines. Sometimes they were chatting, and I imagined how, inside the big old farmhouse, under the supervision of the matron, they cooked and cleaned and nursed other inmates who were sick or dying. They seemed to me to be a family of sorts. I wonder sometimes, if the stigma of the name "poor farm" had been removed, whether these people were not better off, each with work to do within their capacity, than those now idle in their rooms or wards, drugging themselves with television if they are not already drugged with medications.

Were I totally bedridden could I manage to be patient with my caretakers? A close friend of mine, whose passion was gardening, had one of the early cataract operations where the eyes were blindfolded for days and the head had to stay motionless. I visited her in the hospital, bearing a large bunch of flowers and greenery, no two items alike. I spread them out near her hand on the counterpane. Could she identify them by feel and smell? She did, eventually, all but one. And she has never forgotten what that meant to her. She told me later it got her thinking about her thoughts and their colors and their intensities, their odors and their impact, and in the process she began to find out who she was.

She had her flowers. What would I take with me as a symbol to keep close where I could touch or hold it? It would be the bronze hand of a Buddha that was brought to me by my son from Malaysia. The long slender fingers are held in ritual gesture, the nails finely sculptured; and in the palm is a twelve-pointed star. This hand would be, for me, the comfort of the past, of a son's love, of our child-rearing and a passing on of faiths; of our self-denial over the years; and a flowing into the immemorial search of man for his soul and for wisdom and for peace. For I would be holding something once worshipped as a way of loving-kindness and life.

Without that symbol I wonder, if I were limited to a bed and disregarded as a sentient human being, if I could keep my serenity. I doubt it. There would be too much rage in me. How reduced must one be to acquire a totally non-assertive simplicity and humility yet avoid apathy? Nurses can, if ruthless, raise hell in those they deal with. Or would I gently touch my hand of Buddha and let my thoughts be the long, long thoughts of pure patient old age?

One simple thing made me decide to stay on in my own house: my need of solitude. By hook or crook I would stay independent until the last possible moment. I must be ill indeed if, through grit and guts, I could not manage. By little touches of neatness I could keep the house attractive even though my bed didn't get made. Dust didn't matter. Way back when my leg was in a cast almost to the thigh, I could get in and out of the tub and fix Alec's meals, from a wheelchair that had a fine big tote bag hanging from the handle. Of course I could care for myself! And help was available: visiting nurses, Meals-on-Wheels . . .

No, no nursing home. Die in my own house as had my parents . . . And now came back the memory of my father's death that I had put aside as among the imponderables, out of mind, yet never to be forgotten.

When he was eighty-four Father had a massive stroke. He was cared for at home. He was tube-fed. He responded to nothing. Mother often went in silently to look at him and went out again. Two months after the stroke he developed an embolism in one leg. The condition grew worse. Amputation? In a joint decision by Mother and us four children, all life-prolonging measures were removed. Now it was only a matter of waiting, and my sister and I stayed there with Mother as the time began closing in fast. One night I slipped down in dressing gown and bare feet. It was the twenty-third of June, and I sat on the opposite side of the bed from the old, capable, gray-haired nurse. She had little to do but inject morphine every four hours and wait. And as we sat through those long hours, I sometimes recited the *Bab Ballads* and/or sang, off-key, bits of the Gilbert and Sullivan operettas, as Father had done with us children. Of course he couldn't hear but I needed to recapitulate something. Terrible harsh breathing would come from the bed, then he would not inspire at all until some signal in the brain clicked on, and then the great rasping gasps would begin again—on through the night.

The nurse and I drank coffee periodically and had a midnight snack. I led her to talk about herself, her upbringing, her faith, and her belief in the sacredness of life itself even if it were a mindless, soulless life. In a leisurely way I asked about her reasons for going into nursing originally; I drew out her compassion for those who suffer, her need to nurture and to heal; I compared that healing to the final great healing of death, and at last I asked her if she could give a fatal dose of morphine that would end Father's suffering and take him to God.

We sat in silence. The faintest light was beginning to come into the room. Across the bed from each other we waited, the nurse's finger on Father's pulse. Finally she said, "There."

I kissed Father's forehead and walked out through the door to the porch where we children used to swing in the hammock and the phoebe always flew off her nest above; and I stepped onto the lawn and a descendant of our childhood phoebe flew off as usual. The sun broke over the horizon and turned the dewdrops on the grass into a million diamonds. There was a scent of roses in the air; the birds were singing gloriously, and as I paced quietly up and down the lawn my feet made dark prints in the glittering grass. And suddenly I knew a beauty and a glory so tremendous and so wildly uplifting that I felt reborn; and I knew that it would never come to me again unless perhaps at the moment when I in turn should die. I could have said I had just killed my father, but the world was transfigured with wonder, and hallelujahs flowed through and around me. I was above and beyond time and space. . . .

Duty called me in from that joy. Later I stood on the porch alone as Mother, with the other three close around her, moved slowly toward the new-mown field and the random haycocks. I knew from the way they walked that they were all bursting with suppressed grief, although nobody cried. Why didn't I join them? The spirit of my loving, gentle, steadfast father was beside and within me, and I must be alone a little longer with that transcendent feeling to fix it in my soul. And in that short time all fear of human death seemed to pass.

CHAPTER 12

Summer was at hand. I felt as if I was standing and rapping at the great door of the great unknown. But I didn't know which side I was on or whether I was trying to get in or trying to get out. *Was* there any wisdom in insecurity?

To the beach again—at last, that family place on Cape Ann where generations had summered and expanded for over one hundred years. The beach where I was born in 1900 (dirt cheap—delivery fee was fifteen dollars) and had my being every summer for fifty-eight years until Mother's death. Alec then said, "No more." For he had no affection for my affection for my relatives. A few years before he himself died, I had been able to buy the house I was born in, and I rented it on a long-term lease to friends, who took charge of everything so I had only to pay bills. I never had to leave Alec and go down there.

But my nostalgia, increasing with each year, was now an intense craving. The place, I felt, must hold healing for me. And this summer the house—my rather run-down 1850 cottage—was no longer under lease, but was *mine* at last.

I took in great gulps of the tangy salt air as I got out of the car. I had been thirsty *so* long. My eyes stretched to where, that silent-hot day, there was no demarcation between sea and sky. And that night the sweet air curled in and around my bedroom and let me sleep. But I was not yet able to see it as my house but as a house I was visiting. For I spent my time mostly in bed or, pad on knee, feet up, lying on a chaise on the porch. I dreaded each trip over the banister-less stairs. How, *how,* did the full- and long-petticoated and -skirted women of old navigate this steep and narrow channel? After tripping all over myself, I held the hems of my nightgown and dressing gown in my teeth as I mounted. When the absurdity of it hit me, I cut off the hems at the knees.

Summer for me was a matter of staring hungrily, day after day, out at the curve of the cove, the point of the island, at sea and sky, changing weather patterns with their slight responses in my body.

Summer was, for me, walking with cane, just once, down the cliff path to the little beach and back by the long gradual route. (Just once. Only once. Never again, I vowed.) It saw the arrival in my bedroom or upstairs porch at about five o'clock each night of relatives and friends, bidden or unbidden, carrying up the evening drinks.

Summer was the coming of my western family of six (plus boy friends) arriving in varying stages. Since every one of my individual clan—twenty-three in all—was around at one time or another, I sent out word at last that I was "closeted" until around noon and again after lunch till around five. People exhausted me.

This was all the more perverse because, earlier in the spring, bound copies of my book about the family had arrived, and I had touched them with awe, and numbered them, and grown a cubit in stature. Inevitably relatives visited me more often this summer because of the book. Some came to congratulate (rarely to criticize), many to reminisce on their own childhoods there. And sometimes young relatives brought visiting friends to "meet" me.

Admiringly, I gather. It made me want to do something ridiculous. Once there were five of them sitting almost in a row before me. As they looked at me, all eyes fixed, waiting, they seemed to be saying, in effect, "Give!" The impulse came for me to say, as if to little birds, "Open!" and for them, like little birds, all in turn to open their mouths wide and be fed predigested worm. I was not used to being on display.

This summer a newspaper reporter interviewed me there on the porch, and it was pleasant, I found, to talk about myself without guilt for once, though I was guarded. And then a day or two later, came a news photographer. I am one of those who collapse into some morass of guilt and embarrassment when a camera is pointed at them. So, after sitting on the end of the low stone wall before the water, stiffly smirking and trying not to, I said to the young man suddenly, "Tell me the very worst thing you ever did in your life."

He lowered his camera and stared at me in disbelief and misery.

"No, I mean it. It'll take my mind off."

He looked out at the water for a moment. "I tailgated a policeman in an unmarked car and then I sassed and argued with him, and then—" he groaned but warmed to his rather nasty story, and while I listened entranced, his fingers by habit did their work. Smart young man! It was the only good picture ever taken of me.

One part of my mind seemed stronger that summer, even as I was feeling worse and more utterly helpless. For I was discovering depths, having ceased simply to observe and remark on myself. More and more was I utterly obsessed by other people who were as old and miserable as I was. I must write to them so they would know they were not totally alone. I must write to them—and to myself.

Yet there were times that summer that promised chaos. If I were getting myself a meal I would stand bewildered in the middle of the kitchen. I didn't know where anything was in that house of mine anyhow, not yet. I was too fragile, splintered, confused, too impotent after my isolated silent year, to reorganize. And so much dismayed me. When the young were there, thoughtful and loving though they were, the kitchen wastebaskets seemed constantly full of empty unflattened cartons, boxes, bottles, beer cans; the icebox full of God knows what, the washing machine going, the clothesline full. And the showering! Everyone, every day, or twice a day to clean off the lovely salt from the sea. And the hair washing and blow-drying, a telephone call, a leap out the front door, a car going down the drive . . .

A part of me asked, How can you get angry at grandchildren who sit by your bedside and tell of their loves and their lives and their hurts, and who always say, arriving or leaving, "Anything I can do for you, Grandma?"?

But I did get angry and knew it was my problem. I was jealous as hell of the swift eager freedom of youth—that freedom I had not known at their age. Yet not for anything would I be young again with all my growing pains ahead. And it was—was—now I began to see—it was the generation gap in my dedication to the aging while living among so many of the young. And having thought it out, I again felt my patience and the gentle waiting of the old. And each night I sat motionless on that porch off my bedroom and watched the night lay itself down upon the sea.

Settled again into the winter patterns, smoking constantly, body-listening, clock-watching for the moment for pills that gave no real relief, still preferring isolation, I tried to deepen concentration. Misery out of fatigue, fatigue out of misery, no crash courses, heady stuff, the world empty, and I in my own Black Hole.

There was one day when I was fairly desperate with pain, and the feeling came that no one on earth was thinking of me, was consciously aware of my existence there on my bed at that moment. I flinched at the enormity of creation. Billions of stars in the billions of galaxies billions of light years away and constantly moving apart at incredible speeds or sucking together so furiously they flew and fused into nothingness. Of course God had no time to note the sparrow's fall. I was utterly alone, unknown-of and therefore an un-being. And a dreadful shock of emptiness rose to an almost screaming pitch of tension—alone, nobody, nothing, not even any palpable I. And suddenly my body and I seemed to take off into space in an emotional pain that, strangely, dissolved into a moment of exquisite beauty, a flowing into the infinite and the forever. Existential ecstasy? I wondered if dying felt like that.

Another time, when my old mind had

been very open, I knew cold fear, an appalling, horrible, terror-fear. Fear of what? Quick I tried to trace it. Omen of dire sickness? I knew that twinge. Being-found-out anguish of childhood? No, this was different. Fear of my own uncontrolled murderous rage? No again, I'd tackled that. Fear of sudden violent death, as to an animal in the wild? This had self-awareness in it. Terror of the Gods, the unknown, the retaliatory? Nearer, but not yet it.

I could perhaps compare it to the freeze I always feel when a foot from behind jars the rung of my chair unexpectedly, opening up in me a crack to the animal terror of earthquake. I used to be suddenly furious when that happened. Did this fear go back, back to the time when man was achieving a conscious mind, and with it fear of raw evil, sorcery, magic, and mystical uncontrol that becomes madness? Was this the kind of fear that can, in very rare situations with primitive or superstitious people, bring on a sudden inexplicable death out of the sense of being utterly possessed, bewitched, or doomed?

I don't know. I wondered if I could ever see a beauty in it as I had in my existential loneliness. I wondered if, in going to meet that fear without recoil, flowing into it, I could quietly die at my own appointed moment. I could at least see where it would lead me.

Or was this fear a fear of death? *Was* I afraid? There seems to be a fear of being totally alone at the moment of dying. We're going from light into utter darkness. Just as at birth one comes from darkness to light—a light which must seem dazzling. And for the newborn infant as well as the dying old, there is a sudden cessation of acute pain. For the pain of birth can be as acute and intense for child as for mother. (Birth was once simpler, as with other mammals, before the human brain had developed to such large proportions that the pressure and squeezing in the birth canal must have caused agony.) We know that the skull itself sometimes undergoes such pressure that it is misshapen. So I wonder, when someone is unreasonably afraid of death, if perhaps an unconscious memory or sudden flashback to birth is not still active as a deep threat, not only from the individual's own infantile experience but from the collective unconscious, when a journey is made into the totally unknown.

Once when I was in very deep physical

pain I wrote down, without mental censorship, whatever came to mind. I found myself describing my birth. And in that time of misery and anxiety the description came out so vividly and, it seemed to me, realistically, that afterward I stared at what was on the page. I had written something I never knew before. Cannot such deep flashbacks be equated with the reports in Raymond Moody's *Life after Life* and other such books? There are descriptions by individuals of their few moments of declared death. I put together, out of context, some of the remarks: entered head-first into a long dark passageway; the tight tunnel; the squeezing and pressure; the sudden radiance; the cessation of pain; the figure in white; the hand beating on him. This would in no way negate the belief in life after death, but one can perhaps equally equate it to conscious life during birth.

Before I started studying old age I used to think that I would want and need no succor or pity at my ending. Now I hope that caretakers will be tender with me, and that friends and relatives will follow my lead, touch me, scold me, tease me, laugh, cry, and rejoice with me. Why not? I don't always want to have to hide myself.

There was a third imponderable for me to consider. Periodically through recent years I had known a little space of immemorial sadness, far beyond any individual grief or bereavement. At man's unavailing search for surcease? At lack of stillness of mind day or night? At never finding any ultimate reason to life and death? For lost innocence? The cry of man without the God that he made him? The eternal struggle with the very pain of living with emotions?

None of these moments of intensity, all akin in one way, could find an object or focus or purpose. They didn't belong to me or to my mind. Did they live in my limbic system?

It seemed to me there was one companion only to such sensations—death—and that man's mind and death walk hand in hand from the moment a child discovers himself as a self. Man discovered knowledge in the Garden of Eden when he bit into the apple: was this not a myth for the time man (or child) first found, made a word for an object? Up to then he floated in a state of simple purity in nonseparateness from anything else—sun, moon, the elements, plants, and animal life. But with the word he had formed for that object he looked from himself to that thing and found it was apart from him, and he looked at himself, and now he was no longer innocent (as is the lion with its antelope or the spider with its fly). The need to kill was no longer a simple survival instinct, it was a wish; and he knew shame, and he put on clothes of pretense to cover himself from his own eyes and sin began. He had to invent God. "In the beginning" (said man) "was the Word."

Man had achieved a brain that thought and watched itself think: from thing to concept to symbol to myth.

I saw that a creative impulse could arise from the meeting of the predictable and the unknown to produce a new image, and vice versa; or from the sudden unconscious connection of diverse symbols in a liberaton of vision even if not yet a liberation of insight, or from a sudden departure from the obvious, or in the expulsion of a cry out of a racial past or in the bloom of a mystical vision.

So I saw how mind has to use mind to know itself. I saw that the made object must be faithful to the inner truth of the one who creates. I saw that the more that creativity is driven by anguish the more perfect and intent it can become. Shakespeare says,

"They breathe truth that breathe their words in pain."

But why the drive or compulsion to create? Why me, at this age? Now it seemed that ever since losing his Eden, man, knowing unutterable longing in his loneliness, his fear, his sadness and his emptiness, strove through art, in whatever form he could master the skills, to make children-things of beauty out of immaculate conception. He was announcing himself. He made his first clay pot with joy and love. And in the making, and in his pride at his finished creation, and for the moment, the abyss of grief and sadness over his lost Eden was forgotten, and he rested from his labors, at peace.

CHAPTER 13

Here in bed I was, hung between pain and what pain can do if one listens. I had prepared, in a tangible way, for my death, I had daydreamed it and imagined it in every possible form, and found my favorite picture was the one of H. G. Wells's last moments. With relatives and friends around trying to get some final response from the great man, he whispered with slight impatience, "Can't you see I'm busy dying?"

I decided to look again, as directly as I could, which would be as one looks through smoked glass at the sun. It was then that death appeared in the doorway. I turned off the TV fast.

He was quite formless at first, merely a misty wraith. I asked, "You've come for me?" I saw a slightly amused smile.

"Certainly not now. You're angry."

"Then why?" He was coming close now, tall, straight, stern, in a great black cape lined in red. I saw him like Alec in his best role, Death, in *Death Takes a Holiday*.

"You called me," he said. "You wanted to see me."

"I don't. I didn't."

"You're always dragging me in and yet you never look at me squarely. Are you afraid of me?"

I thought a moment. "You were kind to Alec. You took him so quickly he didn't know. I've never thanked you. I thanked God instead."

"You're evading."

"You sat with me when Father and Mother died."

"Naturally. I was there."

"Yes, oh, yes! You gave me the kiss that I gave to Mother. You made the diamonds on the grass and the beauty of the morning when Father died. Should I be afraid?"

"You were once."

My mind flashed back and Death waited quietly. I was about three years old. A woman was sweeping the floor and from a corner ran a big bug! A black shoe came down bang. The woman lifted her foot.

"Spider! Got it. Dead!" I squatted to see. It was now flat with hairs of legs sticking out of the sides. "They bite. Look out for them," she said. She swept it into the dustpan.

"Dead." What was "dead"?

In my grandmother's kitchen at the beach there were always cookies in a jar. The cook gave me two and went on mixing batter. There was a flat yellow flypaper on a table. I watched a fly land. Its feet stuck. Struggling, it finally extracted one leg, tried the next, got the first stuck back in, heaved, and fluttered its wings—on and on—then it collapsed flat. It tried once more. The struggle was awful but shorter. Then it lay still and never moved again. Or did the body stir just a little? No more. Dead. It was the fight to live that was so dreadful. I never watched flypaper again.

One spring we incubated our own chicks. On a warm day Mother put them out into a tiny wooden house in the sun. There was a three-inch-high door for them to go out and in, and a small wire yard kept them from straying. We heard a shrill incessant peeping and hurried out. The chicks were all clustered against the wire. Mother lifted off the top of the house and inside was a tremendous black snake coiled up. There was a bulge in the middle of it. The only black chick, mine, was gone.

"Do you remember the time—I was around twenty—when I stood at the top of the hill beyond our old orchard and looked across to the sunset and it was one great fire moving toward me at incredible speed, and I stood very tall and shouted, 'I am ready!'? You were that great thing coming."

Death looked amused. "I wasn't even there. Maybe you were calling me to see if you would be afraid. You always had to force your face to fear."

I felt slightly let down. "Well, remember the times I wanted to go out with the tide or the waves to find you?"

"I stopped you. You didn't want to find me; you wanted to find yourself."

"Well, I knew you were there the time the woman died in the hospital across the hall. She called, 'Mummy.' "

"Sometimes I'm called Mummy, sometimes Lover, sometimes God, sometimes Devil." He stood closer to my bed now.

"I've never looked at you before," I said.

"I'm only what you make me."

"Do you ever punish anyone, like the

jealous gods who retaliate or strike blind?"

"Now really! I've got open arms for anyone who's ready, even if he doesn't know he is, and for those who call me. They let themselves go so gratefully. You're one of those who keep up the good fight, head up, and never let the body and brain rest. Few hear the great sigh of relief at the end. But I know."

"What about war and deliberate killing?"

His face was hard and grim suddenly. "Some men are more bestial than the beasts, and mass killing is bestiality without guilt."

"Well, auto accidents, then?"

"That's one way to find me and yet deny the desire. You can add cigarettes to that." He pointed to my full ashtray.

"What do you do with bodies?"

"Bodies? I don't. You're mixed up like everyone else and you're talking about death with a small *d*. Nature or morticians handle death, which is what man does to himself or others do to him or his genes command. The great old tree at last falls in the forest, a rabbit is fox-eaten, plants are destroyed by overwatering, and an old, old dog goes off by himself to drop down quietly to wait. Degeneration, corruption, regeneration." Now he spoke rather proudly: "I'm Death with a capital *D,* the so-called enemy of man, the Grim Reaper, created by man out of his own fear."

"But why such fear?"

"Failure. People are afraid of insubstantiality because they've never really been substantial. They never looked inside themselves. And loss, yes, loss of an imperfect self which hates itself; loss of another chance which wouldn't be taken anyhow; loss of the last opportunity to get and give love. They're as afraid of the fear of meeting what they imagine me to be as they are of the fear of living or of dying."

He looked away, eyes sad and unfocused. "The joke of it is, I don't exist. I'm a state of mind; ugly, terrifying, or beautiful, depending on each person. Those who can't relax feel more fear, and more pain in their dying. They trust nothing. I watch all the rituals of avoidance with grim humor. They're everywhere, both before and after death. But those who sit easy to life die well."

"Can you love?" This was an important question to me. His face became inspired and filled with beauty, his smile incredibly sweet. I saw Alec's fine face the way I saw it at certain special tender times when he looked at me, and the way I saw him as

Death when he said to the lovely young girl who wanted to return with him to his domain of the dead, "My love! My love! My little love!"

"I know," Death said, not needing to say yes or no.

For the moment I didn't want to think. I wanted only to feel that love. The longing to lie so safe beside his strong warm sleeping body was incredibly poignant.

I sat up straight and looked intently at him. "What about my damned back? Will it finish me off in the end?"

"You've been having a hell of a good time with that back of yours—no, don't interrupt—writing, discovering, growing, isolating yourself where no one can bother you or make you mad. Now face it. Move on. Pain makes the brain squirm. How do you think man evolved? Birth pain, life pain, death pain, all part of the struggle to become man. Not random mutation, not survival of the fittest but the struggle to avoid pain that animals can turn off but man can't except in emergencies—fight or flight. So you've changed and grown. Next step. A leap. Get out of bed."

"How, where?"

"You'll find a day and a way." He began

to disappear slowly, grow more misty, but the smile lingered.

"Don't go, don't go! One more thing. What about life after death? I want no part of it."

There was a motion like a shrug of what was left of the mist. "Remember that everything is a state of mind, and that can become a need."

"No, listen! Hold it!"

"You listen first. When you finally call on me in trust and sincerity and real readiness, I'll come if . . . doctors don't interfere."

"I can't see you any longer but I know you're there. I'll leave my ivory tower when I can find a way. Wait—I'll be quick. I've got a ridiculously silly idea. It's what I want after death—my ashes to be scattered off the island at the beach, with bits of bone among them like Alec's, and one or two of those bits to be washed up on the sands with an on-shore wind, and my great-grandchildren to be playing right there where I first found myself as a child—and one of them to pick up a bit of bone and look intently at it and yell, "Hey, everybody! You kids! Come quick! I've found a piece of Grandma!"

The voice came out of nowhere and nothingness but it held laughter. "That's all right, too."

My fantasy with Death must have opened another hard-locked door. That night I had a nightmare, a horrible, horrible one, and woke in whirling terror to some awfulness of memory. I, a small child—dancing from sunlight into the dimness of my grandmother's barn . . . the stablehand . . . rough, rough dirty hands . . . Then sunlight, and a clinging to the strong upright bar of my brother's stroller as the nurse walked us home.

The next night, again in wild restlessness, another dream of agony and then more memory. Mother—Mother looking at me! And Mother's face! There was killing in those wild eyes, and the life was struck out of me by that look! I must have been terribly bad if she wanted to kill me!

I had regained a true, if partial, memory at last and it filled in a picture that had eluded me for seventy years, even throughout analysis. But many cover memories, little habits, many incidents attested to its truth. Now I knew an incredible relief. I rejoiced. But why, then, was I still afraid somewhere inside?

Where was my wise woman now in this

heavy-bodied flatness of mine, giving out nothing? Where that peaceful ending of which the late lark sings? For that poem no longer held its magic. A new daydream came. Well, not quite a daydream: a cry, rather. A craving to sit loose, let go, be a child again, in the purest sense. I wanted so, before I died, to hear my own true voice (for I must have one), and no longer be a watchdog to myself according to the guardianship of my ancestors. To get angry, yet know that anger would flash out and be done. To know grief, and cry, and smile again. To ask why the wind, to *be* the wind. To ask why I, yet need no answer.

I've seen faces in life, in art, of great or unknown men or women or saints: faces that are childlike and radiant, innocent yet bright with high intelligence, unself-conscious faces in their simplicity and clarity, faces that suggest a touch of wonder at the world, and a great compassion for all who suffer, since they too have suffered. How joyous to be utterly relaxed, to do something innocently dumb and laugh merrily at myself; to glow with unrestrained humor and whimsy; to see crazy connections that the rational mind has not yet blocked; to be impetuous and ingenious and ingenuous and joyful inside at all the incredible wonders like cows eating grass. To know that I breathe and that there is one breath in all men, and that I am the world. I, as child again, knowing so much that I can forget knowledge and return home a little space, a little time.

Only so can I go on—flowing into very old age and keeping my very sane sanity even in the subliminal areas of my brain. Only so can I become natural in my body. I know that this old woman could do no one hurt or harm. There would be a kind of fusion between the floodlit simplicity of the retarded child who loves and trusts naturally and the sharp spotlight intelligence where suffering has carried one beyond pettiness and into new depth.

All this I learned for now. My forty days in the wilderness: would they ever be over?

CHAPTER 14

November came, and a visit to my local orthopedic surgeon, desperately following up on his suggestion of eight months before: spinal nerve blocks. He had said they held no special promise. I was referred to a neurosurgeon in the city, and before long a room was available for me in the hospital there. I went without much hope, expecting more pain. I got it.

Almost three weeks in the huge place, days when nothing happened; various doctors in and out; it was all so bad that I remember very little. Hope raised, hope dashed, over and over. The Big Man in once in a while, nothing chatty about him; gray, muted, passive, unsmiling; his henchmen in more often. I too listless to get to know the names. Novocaine, spinal nerve blocks twice, xylocaine once (I can't even remember what the process was or how or where I had it but I didn't like it). Four to six hours of heavenly release and relief. Then pain always returned in full force.

Notification of anything to happen was rarely given. X-rays, exams, blocks, tests between days of waiting. Example: a wheelchair came in. In my pretense at bright cheerfulness, "Where to this time?"

"A body scan."

"What! Why?" Anxiety and quick fear.

"Written orders." Of course no use to ask. So I had a body scan. I was eventually told they were concerned with something on a rib that showed up on the routine t.b. X-ray. Christ! If anyone, but anyone, had considered me as a person of *any* intelligence and asked me *any* sensible questions, or kept me in touch with plans, I would have told them I had bumped my rib against the side of the tub getting out one day and bruised a cartilage or bone.

Another time an orthopedic surgeon walked in without warning. No conversation. He'd read everything in the record, of course. He swung my legs about and then pressed both knees hard against my chest. He was a strong man. *Jeezus!* Agony for two days, no medication touching the nerve pain.

One evening when the Big Man visited he told me he'd asked a psychiatrist to come to see me. Hurray!! So he had *some* sense. The new doctor came and was a *Love*. Questions asked. I talked. I questioned. He questioned. I talked more, and found I could be completely open. He came again a few days later. My only memory of what he said was that I hadn't worked through the loss of my husband (that jarred me), and that I was deeply lonely, and that he would be available at any future time if I wanted him.

The Big Man arrived one night to tell me to take a taxi the next morning to the Boston Pain Unit for an interview with a Dr. A, to see if they felt they could help and would take me. "*What?* What's a pain unit?" The Big Man explained and told me why he was sending me there. I couldn't grasp much except that being accepted represented five weeks' in-patient stay, a long waiting list, and a true sense of hope ahead. The next day, shaky, I dressed, was taxied, elevated myself up to the tenth floor of the big isolated building and was again very open in explaining myself, for, like the other psychiatrist, this one before me was one big sponge. I returned, exhausted, to my hospital and my bed and shut the door.

The Big Man came again that evening. A patient had canceled at the unit, and I could go in on Monday. Huh! Five weeks. I'd miss Christmas and New Year's. Hooray! And I thought, "I'll lie here quietly for the next three days with nobody to bother me about anything and then go over to the unit." But no, my bed was needed. I must go home in the morning.

But instead of looking stern (I now believed it was shyness) and gray and muted (which must be fatigue) and impassive (which could be his brilliant humanistic and scientific mind), the Big Man was wearing his first little smile, which might be satisfaction in getting me into the unit so soon or at having gotten rid of me. But I saw that smile as angelic wisdom and felt him to be extraordinary, the rare neurosurgeon, to have called in a psychiatrist and to be sending me to a place of holistic medicine. In an area where the physical approach to medicine—surgery, neurology, medication, et cetera—had reached such splendid if rigid competence, how did that quiet older man break through the narrow confines of his medical tradition to recognize the need for something more?

I lay curled up on the back seat as my daughter drove me into the Rehabilitation Hospital that Monday morning. But I sat straight up as we approached the isolated, starkly functional building that loomed above the moribund railroad yards of the Boston & Maine. As we went through gates past a watchman in his box, I saw that the whole area surrounding the hospital was one great parking lot complete with high wire mesh fence.

The Pain Unit was an aerie ten flights up, buffeted by the winter wind howling around the building's odd angles. A reception desk-cum-nurses' station, with staff sitting room behind; a long corridor with ten double bedrooms and one single room off it; a single shower and tub to serve twenty-one patients; one pay phone on a wall. There was a large dining room, with six tables each seating four or five and a self-service snack bar in the corner. This one room, I was to learn, served for eating, lounging, reading, games, physical therapy or group meditation (done on floor mats, the tables and chairs pushed aside); for medical grand rounds, for big meetings or the patients' own community meetings; for movies of instruction; for certain classes, training periods, discussion seminars, psychomotor groups, and the entertaining of visitors. Here you could smoke, play the hi-fi, the TV, the radio, and talk loudly all at once.

A narrow solarium held another TV, sofas and chairs for about ten people, and a bookcase that contained one picture puzzle and a lot of old Reader's Digest book condensations. More small conference rooms, social service rooms, and two medical offices made up our unit in general. Throughout it was modern, clean, and attractively decorated.

Here, at the end of the corridor, my room: two beds with their curtains, two closets holding two drawers, a shelf, and wire hangers, two chairs, one comfortable, one rigid, two bedside tables, one basin with mirror, a toilet behind a door, a large sealed window and a glimpse of Boston Harbor beyond the dilapidated hulk of the North Station, once a bustling railway terminal.

Since she was here first, my roommate had the bed by the window and the comfortable chair, both of which I envied her. She was a sweet young woman, immature and withdrawn, thoughtless like a child, and, like a child—like a grand-child—naive and innocent and totally open in her nudity. I found I pulled my curtains to spare her the shock of seeing me in *my* nakedness.

I was to find she had some nuisance value—I had never had a roommate before. In her vague way Elsie had the radio on whenever she was in the room (not too loudly), and crooned to it (not too loudly), or talked to herself but with just enough expression so that for the first week I kept asking, "What did you say?" thinking she was addressing me. She stole time from meetings to sit alone cutting, pasting, painting, or making decals for the big window—or worse, the mirror above the basin. Why did I wait ten days before asking her gently to remove them so I could see to comb my hair? Because she was so childlike it might upset her? Certainly her apology held abject misery. She also upset me enough at night when I so badly needed sleep. Restless, she went in and out of the room well into the small hours, leaving the door open to hall noises every time, and it would wake me, and I would get up and close the door again, over and over. During my meditation or relaxation response hours, I asked, as we were supposed to, if she would go out for twenty minutes. She said, so sweetly and gently, "Oh, I won't disturb you; I'll be quiet as a mouse," and in my irritation I kept listening for her soft movements and her starting to hum and then stopping herself. When Elsie left, prematurely, I was able to acquire the one college graduate for a new roommate. We could have talked out any difficulties, but we had none.

This unit was the last institutional hope for people at the end of their ropes. Those who came here came when nothing else had worked, people whose pain was intractable and sometimes inexplicable. Twenty-one patients had twenty-one staff members: doctors, nurses, specialists in massage and other therapies, social workers, psychologists were all trained in relaxation techniques, meditation, psychological understanding, electrical gadgets, kindness and compassion, and firmness in the face of any lack of cooperation.

Initially most patients had one or more psychiatric interviews, and each of us experienced, at least once a week, therapy with a social worker, in addition to joint sessions with members of our own family; group therapy, psychomotor therapy, occupational therapy, daily group physiotherapy, several forms of meditation-for-relaxation training, and classes or discussion groups about almost everything concerning health: medication, psychological attitudes, jobs, futures, money, even sex—complete with explicit drawings to help the handicapped manage despite their handicaps.

After intensive study of areas of our physical limitations, damage, and pain, we were given special individual exercises, which we were to practice alone twice a day, as we practiced meditation, and training in biofeedback (which helped to accelerate the relaxation learning process by providing sensory information); electrostimulators (useful for blocking the pain experience to the brain) were tested and, if useful, provided to us. (They only made my discomfort worse.) We were given deep massage or whirlpool baths when scheduled, hot or ice packs were available at any time we hurt, and ice massages late evenings and early mornings if they were helpful. (And they helped me a lot.)

We must not leave our floor without signing out. Then we could go down to the lobby or cafeteria or walk within the gates. Even when we had a free minute, we were not to loll in our rooms, much less fall back into bed. We were not allowed to complain to the staff if we had a quarrel with another patient, or couldn't stand our roommate. The rule was: work it out within the patient community.

And we must mingle. We must learn to be part of a community again, we must bond, whatever our individual likes and dislikes, and know what it was to be ostracized and earn our way back into acceptance, learn to modify our behavior toward that group of "others," to say simply, "I'm sorry" and mean it. Ah, that was it! Were we not all dropouts from life in our pain, our use of drugs, our isolaton, our denials and depression and sense of unworthiness?

Here, in this place, I was to live and have my being for five weeks.

On the first day, after giving a long and extraordinarily complete physical health history that included my emotional responses to illnesses and operations, I came belatedly to lunch, and took my tray from the steam cart, a tray filled with a clutch of plastic containers and envelopes. Finicky since my anorexic childhood, I looked down at the institutional food, then quickly up at the twenty other patients, a couple in wheelchairs, several in neck collars, others with canes or crutches. They all looked so uninteresting, so ordinary. My mind did a flashback to childhood, to the little public school, to the village farm children there with whom we did not, should not, could not associate freely. Here I felt as naked and vulnerable as in those childhood days. My gorge rose as I searched for an empty seat. Someone beckoned. And between the doorway and the table where voices welcomed me, a sea change came over me. I became a social worker again. I was safe in professional neutrality. Personal feelings were irrelevant since here before me were human beings in need. It has always hurt me to see people damaged, in pain, or handicapped, though I am no stranger to hospitals, and with age the pity has only deepened. How and where could I help?

How ingenious! Suddenly, I was no longer a patient. Right after lunch came group therapy, seven of us and two leaders almost knee to knee in the solarium. Many a time had I led groups, skillfully, but never had I been a member of a simple, small treatment group where each must bring out feelings about which the group would afford its protection. I had some inner warning that there were unknown areas in me that had to be explored. It was far easier to observe and approve the techniques of the leaders and to abet them in supporting the members in their efforts at expression. Ah, mine was a fine position. I was, as usual, a catalytic agent. But the hour and a half was very long.

I hurt so. All over I hurt so! Physical exam, physiotherapy, X-rays, more groups, the day went on interminably until 9:30 when, nauseated from exhaustion and sheer physical weakness, frightened of myself, warped and arched and in intolerable pain (in spite of my usual medication), I could at last get undressed and into bed. My real trial had begun!

It was at least two days later, wasted days, before I confessed to one of the staff, with tears in my eyes, "I'm wearing two hats, the social worker's and the patient's, and one keeps falling off." My plea for help seemed to me a confession of weakness. But to the staff worker, it was something very different. "You've got to be the patient you are," she said firmly, "or you won't get well. A lot of your back problem comes from always trying to care for or protect or nourish others, and then you get angry when no one's doing things for you. Forget all about the rest and think only about yourself."

Didn't she understand that unless people needed me, I didn't matter? I didn't say this aloud, but she heard me.

"Forget the others and be kind to yourself." She didn't say it aloud but I heard her admonish me, *"Matter to yourself."*

The third day I met with my social worker. At last here was a full role reversal. In spite of what seemed his extreme youth, his ability to convey security, his unfailing instincts, his wisdom, his quietness and loving physical touch were extraordinary. I let go, I wept, I worked. And he never allowed me any escape.

"But you haven't answered my question yet, Harriet," he would keep insisting. "You're still running away." And at the end he said that later in my stay I was to bring in certain members of my family for joint sessions. Oh no! That would be difficulty added to difficulty. How to let my children really know what I thought and felt and needed?

It was Friday when I finally called home. I was too bemused and confused to want to, but knew I should. My first words were, to my surprise, "I'm Alice in Wonderland. It gets curiouser and curiouser." I added that it was hard work, it made no sense for any in the family to come in yet, the schedule was too confused, my time too filled, there was no place to chat, and if anybody asked, I didn't want any callers or visitors. "I'm doing very well," I ended, "I think."

Alice in Wonderland. I, Alice, in dreamland, in crazy land, the outside existing only dimly and of no concern whatever. Alice, as I remembered her, sometimes much too big for herself and swimming in her own tears, sometimes so small she almost wasn't; Alice getting to know strange creatures as people and people as creatures, yet feeling as strange and queer herself, never being the same or in the same place twice; Alice, trying to play the game but the croquet mallets as flamingos and the hedgehog balls both defying her control by having awkward wills of their own; Alice, getting bolder and more angry, determined to get the golden key on the glass table, the key that would lead her to the most important place, but always failing to take it when she had a chance and was the right height. But Alice did get through, I remembered, and there, among other strange symbols, was the Cheshire Cat, grinning at her, the grin coming and fading. (Important, that grin. Was it my own, reflected?) And the Red Queen, she of unmitigated hate and fury, who yelled at Alice, "Off with her head!" And though Alice kept running and running, she always remained in the same place . . . until . . .

At the end of the first week, when it was clear that I would stick it out, our community secretary gave me a shiny little child's book and said that we all got one. On departure, she explained, it was the custom to write in it a keepsake sentiment—rather like a high school yearbook. Mine contained bits of doggerel and was entitled "Silver Linings."

The first poem ran:

Though life holds all its treasures out
To be enjoyed by everyone,
It is the lifted face that feels
The shining of the sun.

And the last:

Love and friendship bridge a space,
Make the world a happier place.

To me it seemed so infantile that at the first opportunity I sent it home for my great-grandchild to rip apart.

At this distance I can't fully recall that first week. Its impact was too intense: driving me beyond physical and emotional endurance, making me weak with exhaustion, overwhelming me with the challenge of the new and strange without and within. Did the others feel the same or was it the fact that I was thirty years older than anyone else in the unit?

I remember it as a time of dumb and numb determination, with rare flashes of amusement. There was the group walk outside the compound, escorted by two leaders. Some of us moved fast and some, with canes, slowly, and we dodged traffic, and the winter wind blew papers around our legs, dirt and grit into our faces and noses, and chill into our bones.

Then the ride, en masse, by bus, on Friday night, across town to the YWCA pool. It was bitter cold, the streets filled with Christmas shoppers and lights, and it seemed all quite mad. I, like one out of jail or a mental institution, riding with those people to swim. We, the lame and the halt, doing water exercises under direction (I have always disliked pools, particularly highly chlorinated ones). Then we came back to our self-donated ice cream and cake—a party for children!

And the medication problem. All of us had to be off all drugs before we could leave. The first week you were given what you had when you came in (at least I was). Then warning came that deceleration was beginning. Starting at 8 A.M. we all lined up for our pills and every four hours thereafter, and if we didn't get there within the half hour we didn't get our fix. Very cleverly was deceleration done. You were given a very large bolus, hard to swallow, which contained your entire pharmacological mélange for the next four hours, and day by day there was less in it, until the day I left it contained merely an innocuous filler. For some, really addicted, the process involved withdrawal symptoms; for me it was harmless. One day, for the very first time not aware of pain, I refused my bolus.

"But you've got to take it."

"Oh! Oh? Why?"

"Because you've been rewarding pain

with your codeine and Valium," the nurse said, "and taking the stuff has blocked your body's natural ability to heal itself." I had to think that one over, but I got it. I had watched the minutes and hours, my tension building, my back ever tighter, till the moment when I could take those pills. Then I could relax for a little while, then start the time watch again.

The staff had a fine grapevine system of communication. Each observed; the dossiers grew. It gave me a very warm feeling to know that for once in my life wise and emotionally uninvolved people were studying to understand every single knot in my warp and woof, including the strength of my basic yarn.

Finally I got up courage and energy to descend alone from my ivory tower of institutionalization. A mild winter day. I wanted to be by myself, and in that parking lot, where I walked, watching the cars every minute lest one back out on me, I came to a little spot where there were no cars and no fence, only a bit of lawn, now winter dead, a picnic table and two benches beside the low stone wall, below which lapped a backwater of the Charles River. I looked down into the scum with its rotting scraps of floating wood and at the canal beyond, and thought, longingly, how it inevitably flowed on to the ocean. And my mind went inland to where it all started in some spring of pure sparkling water, the runoff joining another spring runoff and eventually, after passing through pollution, it would all go to the clean and open sea. But there were reflections that still day in my windless corner, and pilings at odd angles, and stones and pilings in reflection are beautiful and magical. From then on I went there whenever the weather was clement and I had any free time—and could escape the women who, seeing me with coat on, clamored to go along too.

There were nights that first week (and even later) when, sleepless for a while in the emptiest hours, I wandered our area, pacing slowly, and usually I met another drooping stray, or one watching TV half asleep, or a couple having snacks and chatting sporadically and listlessly. I would join them for milk and cookies and then go to the windows that overlooked the railroad tracks and the drawbridge, and look down at the row of steady red warning lights there over the cut. Ever and always I seemed to be standing on an upper deck of a freighter, seeing below a large dock, the lights reflected red in gently wavering water, the boat temporarily in the hiatus between one rough sea and another. And where I always so secretly went each time on that little ruminating journey I do not know. But it held deep yearning, a yearning for what was past and a prescience of what might come. For when Alec and I went on freighter trips between my operations, pain always traveled with me.

Sunday came. It was a day of rest and, for me, a day of mental work as I lay propped up on my bed. After the first ten days patients were allowed to leave the hospital once weekly, and those from nearby usually went home or had visitors.

I was doing probably the hardest work I had ever done, for it included (unlike analysis) rapidly stepped up and unwonted physical activity, unwelcome social communication, a straining toward inner understanding, pure hard mentation, and a personality change.

And on that Sunday I worked on my new insight—that sense of intellectual superiority, that innate snobbishness of the "Lady"—and saw suddenly that the greatest of sins was to be too superior to be superior. Bah! but hah! Pride! I had something there! I started a list of my sins and I saw suddenly how superiority had hidden itself, playing out its games with inferiority, subversively and so secretly that my mind had never been conscious of it. So who and what and where was the old sweet, loving, and compassionate I?

I had already said in my therapy group, "I don't need love as such. I've got lots of that in my life. What I need is acceptance on the simplest child's level. What I want is to be me, only me. Help me understand that."

Now I took my own clue and went back in memory. My three favorite fairy stories of childhood came suddenly alive. "The Princess and the Pea," "The Little Match Girl," and "Rumpelstiltskin," and I knew I was all three of them, God help me! The Princess—so exquisitely precious and fastidious that she couldn't sleep when a pea was placed under those twenty mattresses; such sensibility proved she *was* a princess. She must have special treatment. She could then be very gracious. If her cry, "I am a true princess," was disregarded, she would, of course, be too proud to complain. I was always scornful, if envious, of the Pea Princess. Then there was the Little Match

Girl, and many a time I died with her of cold and hunger outside the rich man's warm house filled with rosy laughing children eating their Christmas dinner before a roaring fire: the Little Match Girl, too timid to ask for help, too afraid lest she be refused, who froze to death after her last match went out.

And deep down, deep under her specialness, and her goodness, and her hurt, and her desertion, she was very very angry—and therefore very bad. No wonder wicked Rumpelstiltskin was furious when he was found out, and his secret name—the secret that gave him his power—was spoken aloud. His rage was so great that he destroyed himself—snuffed out in a puff of smoke.

So didn't my superiority cover an insecurity from some wound so deep it was unbearable, so deep it could not be probed and cleaned out, so shameful it mustn't be mentioned? And wasn't my modesty designed to hide my narcissistic demands, a sense of entitlement and destructive rage? It was all a great secret collusion within myself—all very humiliating. No, not humiliating—humbling.

A very sobering Sunday. But I had looked

at my sins and could now go my own way, as naive and helpless and caught as everyone else there, and no more special, just a human in pain and trouble. I, a worm, I, merely another private here, but clean! For the first time since early childhood I had stopped trying to be accepted by being good. For here you were accepted only by being simply human. Alone by a western window I watched a glorious sunset over the Charles River Basin.

Without self-consciousness I now became one of our community. As a body we judged, ostracized if behavior was atrocious (usually the result of anxiety), took back into our bosoms again if a genuine apology came, or even an effort to be pleasant; we protected, depended on, supported anyone frightened or unhappy. We defended one another against the authorities if any of us was in danger of dismissal. This was our family. Love grew. I could lay my head briefly on Mike's shoulder, Benny and I could touch hands quietly, the women and I could embrace. I played fine competitive games of Scrabble with someone I had originally tended to avoid. And Pat, who had helped lay the bricks in this very building, and I had our secret grins and silly jokes. The staff, too, became very dear to me. They were extraordinary people!

At the end of ten days I could go out on leave. I chose the invitation of two friends, a psychiatrist and a social worker, to go to what was then the fanciest restaurant in Boston. I hadn't had that treat in decades and of course I had nothing appropriate to wear! A drive in a deep smooth car through the winter night and Christmas lights, my host assured and tenderly solicitous. Seated at a cozy table, made private with a lot of greenery, and above an enchanting night view, I was as excited as a child at the prospect of luxury and superb food.

The head waiter glided forward. Enormously tall (if he had any brawn he could have made a beautiful dancer), in tails with a great expanse of white waistcoat, he reminded me of Alice's white rabbit at his largest size. I giggled inside, and when he inquired unctuously as to our desires in the way of alcoholic beverages, and solemnly inclined toward this old lady, something got into me. Alice? I made a face at him, I waved my hands, I rolled my eyes wildly and cried, "I've just escaped from a loony bin! I want lots to drink, lots and lots and more and more!" Abruptly he stalked away and we never saw him again. By the time we had stopped our laughter a different waiter arrived and all proceeded decorously and happily in a heaven of gustatorial delight. I was reinstituted and reconstituted, inside and out.

Gradually my back held less and less pain, my legs less numbness, though I still could not sit or stand without constant moving of muscles. I was freer. I grew jaunty sometimes and waggled and high-thighed and swanked. On good days my feet moved out cleanly the way they were meant to. The community was happy with me and for me.

All of us who had pushed on, who had grappled with the demands for change and growth and insight, each within his own capacity, became closer and closer. The warmth was such it was for weeping. We had all been "gentled" by pain, and we felt deep loss as we watched our friends leave, their five weeks done, and looked over the new ones the next day.

And what happened between me and my own children in family therapy? These tense and exciting meetings held little of note yet produced miraculous long-range changes in our relationships. We moved into new deeper levels of openness, of daring to touch, to kiss, to feel understanding. I could let them know I needed them so badly I had had to deny it, I could now tell them what I wanted of them. They could tell me how frustrated they were when I wasn't direct, when I hinted or suggested that this or that needed to be done. Why didn't I ever call or tell them to come? It was like my sweet suggestions to them as children and drove them wild. If I'd only give an order or make a demand, then they knew where they were. As one son said, "Otherwise I sweep everything under the rug."

As they pleaded for clean directness, I felt their true desires. So here was more learning, more wiping away of those areas where an unrecognized anger burned within me and tightened my body and my back. And my social worker wouldn't let my children evade a leading question either. They too squirmed but faced themselves.

My time was drawing to a close. Christmas Day I went home for a few hours, feeling suspended between two worlds, but loving the bath of attention and caring. New Year's Eve we enjoyed, courtesy of the hospital, noisemakers, streamers, caps, decorations, ice cream and cake, and (we couldn't believe it) exactly four ounces of champagne apiece in plastic glasses. Such dissipation! We worked at our jollity. We watched Times Square on TV, we cheered a bit, we kissed one another. But the best was when a few of us, the younger ones, went to the solarium, opened the windows, leaned way out, watched the city fireworks and "whee'd" and "aahed" and shouted to the night, and the better, bigger, and more dazzling the rocket the louder our yells, and the greater our childishness. All ceased at last. I found a little more champagne in a forgotten bottle, drank it to myself, and went to bed. Nineteen eighty had begun.

In this period of my last ten days I summed up, recapitulating my capitulation. What had I learned?

I had learned that my pain was real pain (thank God) and that I would never be totally free of my arthritic nerve-pinching back. But I also learned it need no longer control me, because I could always relax and meditate its spasms away. I had learned that pain creates tension which produces muscle spasm, which produces more pain, then more spasm, on and on, in a merry-go-round. But I discovered that the body knows how to heal itself, given a chance, given release of inner stress. And I learned that long-unused muscles can be regenerated amazingly with the proper exercises, even in the very old. And that human beings have a remarkable ability to control their nervous systems once they know how.

I learned that all of us had to go through a real rebalance of personality, one that held a change of old patterns and an acceptance and understanding of our weaknesses and our hidden sources of anger and hurt. For as a body and individually we had surrendered ourselves to doctors, operations, drugs, and bed, and had become prisoners and passive slaves to suffering. And within this pattern we were all depressed, withdrawn, isolated from people, nonfunctional, often addicted to drugs and obsessed with body symptoms.

I learned that most of us were denying having any life problems, our one concern being our pain. But I discovered that the pain was really a cry for help, which was ordinarily unavailable unless another operation was done, producing more pain, because the cause of the symptoms was often obscure.

At one point a little voice whispered to me, "Don't get well. Think how guilty you'll feel if the whole back problem was nothing at all!" I was already guilty enough to have caused so much worry among my family and concern among my friends. How then could I ask for help?

I learned that guilt and pain are a seesaw. That the pattern for suffering and abuse is set in early childhood but that when anger and aggression are internalized, they work overtime secretly, and within, and always the body is tense in the effort to repress. Depression is like an emergency brake on any direct expression of anger, even though almost to a man we denied it, and insisted that our problem was our pain, not our emotions. And in this context I saw why group therapy was so vitally important, because when one member got insight the group wisdom rose and became therapeutic in turn.

I learned that the onset of pain occurs when psychological defenses are no longer adequate, and I could think back to my struggle for bright and cheerful capability and my eventual failure to keep anger and loss invisible even to myself.

And so I learned why our complicated psychological factors, the pain games that in desperation we worked ourselves into, meant that no help was available to us under the conventional health care systems. I discovered why there was left only one approach—the holistic one—when we must tackle, all at once, all the parts of the psyche-soma functioning, and bring them into harmony.

And I learned, wonderfully I learned, that by a supreme daring in an effort of will one could heal a crippled spirit. And I did dare. I dared to cast off my image of myself as a lovely, controlled, and dignified old lady, cast off all self-respect, all personal privacy, all sense of shame.

It took days of inner dialogue. "I can't!" "It's your one chance, be nobody again. Touch rock bottom." "But I can't. I'm terrified."

For three weeks I had watched that Wednesday night workout in the psychomotor group. One of them had been violent—a woman raging against her whole family in a burst of fury and accusations. (I wondered how much it really accomplished.) A second time nothing much happened: two patients tried but hurt and anger were confined to descriptive words—and their bodies were uninvolved, no immediacy or intensity. The third—a man cried out the loss of his mother when he was three and his father's blaming him for her death, these details for the first time recalled to his memory.

I had read the book *The Primal Scream,* I had known how important it was, if one could, to open the mind and the mouth to the suppressed cry, had seen it with my clients in a more subdued form, but my anxiety built up, for now *I* was the one to scream unless I turned coward. Oh, how easily I could have begged off.

But I came into the psychomotor group, ten of us and two staff members around the great pile of pillows that lay waiting in the center of our circle for any variety of expression, and I said, "I'll try it tonight." And I chose from the group two to represent a supportive and loving mother and father, and two other parents against whom I might direct my hostile feelings.

Then as I stood there I split emotionally. I found myself listening to a woman speaking, a woman who was myself but removed from me. And this woman mentioned having been molested by a drunken stable hand when she was five, but that that was not important compared to the reaction of her always gentle mother. And she described the distortion of her mother's face, the wild, tortured, raging face of the Victorian female who lived in terror of anything possibly

sexual. And that face, the woman said, had haunted her all her life because, though she never knew what sin she had committed, she was irrevocably and unforgivably evil forever and must atone into eternity. She knew she was bad because she was treated differently.

And then came the breakthrough. The woman I was, but was watching in horror and in awe, began to yell uncontrollably, "Set me free! Let me go! Stop looking at me that way! I didn't do anything! I didn't mean it if I did!" (And I kept saying inside, "Go on, go on, don't stop now!") And she began to shout and rave out her rage and spew out her hurt and anger. "I hate you! I'll kill you. You always controlled me, watched me, made me guilty, made me sick. You knew every thought I had. Oh, Father, Father, why didn't you do anything? You always sided with Mother!"

And I watched her utter abandonment to rage, to pain, to anguish, to terror, to tears as she drove one hour of horror out of a child's life.

And finally the primitive cry subsided, and I and that emotionally abandoned alter ego fused again and I was trembling uncontrollably, completely limp and

exhausted and ashamed and beautifully clean and at peace in the knowledge that my incubus of my own making had gone forever. And I felt physical arms around me, and all the others seemed to be crying too.

And now I could grasp something more: that since, in my child's hour of supreme need I could not cry to Mother and receive her love and mercy because of her own agony, I could never trust fully an implacable Mother-God. There was no certain Goodness.

It was almost time to leave now. Several weeks before, I had begged for another of the little books that I so scorned at first. I now took it around to all my friends and wrote my farewells in their books too. Theirs to me were so emotional, sincere, loving, admiring, and so very grateful for virtues I wasn't aware of that I bowed my head. I hadn't tried for those. I hadn't tried for anything at the clinic after the first few days. I quote only one, from a staff person.

Dear Harriet: a poem by Emily Dickinson.
we never know how high we are
till we are asked to rise
and then if we are true to plan
our statures touch the sky.

the heroism we recite
would be a normal thing
did not ourselves the cubits warp
for fear to be a king
With much thanks for your wisdom . . . P.

I received two more gifts in that hospital. Although I had always tried not to inhale, forty years of smoking two to three packs of cigarettes a day had meant considerable intake of nicotine and any attempts to break the habit had brought acute anxiety, stomach pains, and the threat of an ulcer. One day I found myself, cigarette in hand, looking thoughtfully at that lovely slim white cylinder. But I laid it down quietly as the words suddenly leapt to mind, "You can stop now." That was my last cigarette. Body-mind tension no longer craved the countertension of that symbolic pacifier. (In April, 1981, having become intensely curious, I called the research department of the Pain Unit. Confirmation came: the hospital records showed that I had voluntarily given up smoking the very day after my catharsis in the psychomotor group. *Now* I could understand why I had been able to break the habit so simply and painlessly.)

The other gift was a "Fuzzy." These were small soft-stuffed animals, presented with a speech by our community president-pro tem to each leaving patient. In my early days I had put "Fuzzies" in the same category as the little book—childish. But now, the evening before I left, I sat, a nice ordinary everyday individual among the nice ordinary everyday others, all of us unordinary to ourselves, all made kind by pain, and I waited with expectancy as if I knew I would understand something more. And I did. As my soft rabbit (!) was put in my hands, as unusual words were spoken, I knew that the Fuzzies were more than a reward to a well-loved child in a close-knit family, more than a security blanket for us to take from the training nursery into a world where we would have to test ourselves again and again, where society and jobs could present problems for many, where sabotage was possible in families not entirely pleased to have roles changed and no invalid available for projection.

No, the Fuzzy and the child's book were symbols out of group wisdom, wisdom that is always greater than the sum of all its individual wisdoms (it always amazes me when I see it in action), and that wisdom spoke. "Dare to be childlike. Dare to hug and cuddle. Dare to laugh and have fun, and be naive and simple and joyous at heart. Dare to be free. Hallelujah."

I came in as a lady of one kind. I left as a woman. And I had found that blood can wash away blood.

The last day I tried to say it all in a letter to the head of the Pain Unit:

> To step aside from the instincts and knowledge of a professional mind, and to be honest, simple and simply honest as a nobody on the path to humility. To be aged, yet young at heart among the young, and to adjust to their ways.
>
> Used to commanding life, now to take orders and obey rules; spoiled, yet grateful for things heretofore scorned.
>
> To listen endlessly and not speak of self; hear gripes and not become involved; have twenty children in pain to touch and hold and caress, yet be a child among them.
>
> To discover the chinks in one's armor, long since made solid with age, and then tear them further open; to spill one's guts before all the young around one, and find that with their help and love the wounds healed.

To lose face to oneself and glory in it, albeit ruefully; to glory in the discovery of new areas of growth.

To have five weeks with hardly a creative thought and to find in that innocence and clean space a new freedom from conscience and the old self-at-home.

Above all, to feel the iron bands of pain and spasm drop gradually from one's body and to walk free and tall once more, breathing lightly and ready to take that long last march and enjoy its myriad and subtle delights to the full.

Thank you, Dr. A.

From an Octogenarian

I was no longer Alice in Wonderland as I left. I was normal size at last. For had I not myself shouted at the raging Red Queen, at the jury, at my other fears, "You're nothing but a pack of cards!" And the cards had flown about frighteningly for a moment and then collapsed, flat.

As one doctor son said, incredulous at the change in me, "What's the matter with us in the medical field anyhow, that we're so blind?"

CHAPTER 15

My daughter and her family had taken sanctuary in my house for some weeks while I was hospitalized. (They were waiting for delayed completion of their new house in another state.) It was still Christmas vacation for the three college-agers when I returned home. My bedroom was shining and welcoming. The rest of the house was—well, with three beds it was hardly equipped for six. I had told the family to make themselves at home. They had.

At this point in my healing I needed order and control. And one night as I went to bed I was so frustrated and angry that I thrashed myself to sleep. But I woke to a dream and found myself saying out loud, "Pass the predictability, please!" That was my father teaching us children table manners in his relaxed voice—and that, as I laughed at my own whimsy, was the end of the irritation. I flowed with the tide until I had the house to myself again and could reorganize and return everything to its wonted place.

Habit now became pure pleasure. At whatever time my mind and the light woke me I stretched to the morning, for I could stretch now. Window closed, thermostat up, the bathroom routine accomplished—including a long and lingering hot tub soak—the kitchen welcoming, everything spoke to another fresh day and new beginning. Water sang in the small kettle, instant coffee and sugar went into the mug. Juice or fruit, raisin bran (or whatever) in the bowl with cream and brown sugar on top. I opened the front door and breathed deeply the frosty morning air that prickled the nostrils, picked up the unfailing newspaper, settled back in bed with the tray and read what news I wanted. Then, what should this day be? Anything. Mine to play with and to write in. And when the day was over and I laid my head down on the pillow I was, as Alec used to be, at once into sleep without knowledge of the passage.

Softly and secretly at first I tested over and over my new strength and freedom, often doing too much physically and having to lie low for a bit. Also four or five times daily in my new housework activity I retired to my comfortable bed position and worked on relaxation and breathing. And always pain went and I rebounded.

Faithfully I did the exercises as prescribed by the Unit for my back and legs, did therapeutic pool swimming, walked daily, weather permitting, began yoga but gave that up until I was wiser as to what I could and couldn't do. Motion must be constantly tested for the pure pleasure of it. Moving around the house, I felt like a child after school, sometimes flinging up my arms to feel muscles, or windmilling them, just to show off to myself, sometimes sashaying along the floor, or rotating my hips and whole body to music, swinging and swaying, or jogging in place or even trying a very old jumprope. (That clearly was beyond my power of self-elevation as yet.)

It seemed as if my car whinnied its welcome, and sometimes I drove just to drive, watching details of winter landscape never noted before. The front seat now fitted my back perfectly. I was like a sixteen-year-old first taking the car out alone.

Clothes-shopping was possible once more, in real shops, not just mail-order catalogues.

I could stand straight now and hold my belly in fairly well. Except for housecoats I had bought nothing new for several years. I indulged. It amused me to think that, were I ninety years old, I could pick the same model as the twenty-year-old—this in deep contrast to my youth, where each age had its distinct style. I wanted to be pleasing to my own and others' eyes and I distinctly preferred bright red for color, even buying rosy red sheets for my bed. I chose dresses with softness so I needn't wear the always-hated bra and girdle that bound me, however lightly. And I took to perfume (ha, "Joy") again, two bottles unused for decades.

Entertaining people? I could now do it, if modestly, on tiptoe. The day for gay dinners is past when you're eighty. But the cocktail party—that's possible because it's time limited, or, if it goes on and on it means we're all having a hell of a lot of fun. For such entertainment every last thing is pre-prepared, all liquor supplies attractive on the dining room table, canapés placed strategically, fire lit, candles glowing, lights dimmed, then guests arrive, and as I welcome them I say, "Would you make your own drinks and get a second for anybody who has a thirsty look." I come up for air once in a while to check on supplies but am generally invisible as a hostess. Happy as a guest at my own party.

Cooking was amazing after my long years of dearth of tasty food, for Alec's preferences had been dull and repetitious and any new taste or article was rejected. And I first as widow, then as semi-invalid, cooked the minimum. Now I beheld anew the varying shapes, sizes, qualities, consistencies and colors of so many substances—and these could be knifed, blended, processed, pounded, fused, stirred, patted, or rolled and eventually be exposed to heat (liquid, steam, dry, or radiant) or to cold, moderate or intense, and the end result would be, with perhaps a few more swift hand motions conveying herbs, changed magically to beautiful new sights, tastes, and textures on the tongue.

I played bridge again (after forty years I had to learn the new conventions) but my card sense was only enhanced by its long dormancy—the pips on the cards so clean, the anticipation so rich as each new hand was dealt. I was a gambler at heart. The theater—to sink into the soft seat as magic from the past flowed into me and I was, in that ambience, uncritically open to any potential impression as the lights slowly dimmed. At parties, small ones, I found self-consciousness had melted away. I said whatever came to mind, naughty and twinkly and sassy. Where had my old reserve gone?

The children all remarked on the lilt in my voice when I answered the phone, and I found myself saying, to family or close friends, as I hung up, "Love you." I felt simple, as if I worked out of a unified center. Now I could show my gratitude to those who stayed loyal even when I reacted so thinly and sometimes rejected offers. In a very bad time one could say, in effect, "Don't ask too much of me. Bear with me a little while. When I'm ready I'll give in return." I myself should have said that more openly, but I was ashamed.

We all need others, even the misanthrope has to have people to hate, otherwise he feeds on himself. And I've known elderly bitter bickering couples who talked divorce but who would never take that step, for whom would they then have to be furious at or to fight with? However much I may talk to myself or look at my image in the mirror, I'm not attested to and validated unless there is some relationship that holds reciprocity.

In old age we have learned through time and experience to recognize when someone is mentally honest. We are all skilled in the art of the little white lie—and we may be startled or hurt by the brusque female who refuses to toss one into the air to create pleasure. The complimentary lie we accept with reservations, but with the pleasant knowledge that an attempt is being made to make us feel good.

Until trust is fully established there can be tensions with all of the subtleties of the unspoken which can be read only through nonverbal clues. And these I must search out. Or I can make a frontal attack. Blake says so simply in "A Poison Tree."

I was angry at my friend.
I told my wrath, my wrath did end.
I was angry at my foe,
I told it not, my wrath did grow.

Sometimes it helps to be frank. True friendship is both lovely and delicate and it is to be respected and cherished. Clean love contains that great gift of sensitivity to another's pain. If my love is not greedy, if my lovingkindness is true, I will develop a listening ear, listening without giving advice or criticism, and will know intuitively when to talk or when not to, and how to stop another's flow of words before it becomes too private and intense. For people feel guilty and then angry when they expose themselves too much. And when we do receive confidences, even our minds must be sealed.

If we try to ask parental nurturance from other people, except in brief periods of extreme need, we are likely to lay too much responsibility on them. And since our lives are more restricted, there can grow up an intensity of intimacy that is too heavy. If friends sense a hunger in us they know they cannot fulfill, the reaction is often to withdraw. For in our possessiveness we may be asking them to be indulgent as a parent, or as obedient as a child, and to give as ceaselessly as in a parent-child relationship. We may also become jealous, which is a terrible burden for a friend to bear. On the other hand we must not get involved in the intense emotions of others or become so troubled that we side with them strongly and without judgment. There's a trick of sorts to this that I learned in social work training and have ever since used in any steep or rough relationship. I mentally shift gears, going from high, where I am running spontaneously and impulsively, down to second, which says, "Caution, watch it, long down grade," or I move even into low, low gear, "very steep grade, curve at bottom," and am now in a ratio that leaves me comfortably holding myself back against the pressures and drag of a friend's emotions, and so able to keep steady control on my own impulses.

We must not feel betrayed if a friend withdraws suddenly or turns against us. First, in my case anyhow, I have to consult myself. Were my demands too heavy? Was I pressing too hard? Next, "What the hell is she up to?" Or, "What the hell am I up to?" And finally, I think of Longfellow's remark, "If we could read the secret history of our enemies, we should find in each man's life sorrow and suffering enough to disarm all hostility."

Some of the worst suffering occurs during early bereavement and I thought back to what I had needed and what I had learned and how I would ideally react with another widow. I'd refer to the deceased by name easily and almost at once. I'd show silent sympathy in an attitude of readiness as if I were listening to a frightened child: I'd open the door to communication with a "Tell me about it if you can," or even, "What hurts most?" I'd be in readiness to hear details, however distressing, about the dying process, the funeral and any family disagreements. When I sensed the time to be right, I'd give a touch of caring or a kiss, or hold closely. I'd accept comfortably any outbursts of grief, rage or recrimination, but I'd quickly reassure that whatever was said would never be repeated. There might be an angry attack on myself, and I'd take it without reaction, and when I left I'd say that I'd be back if my friend would like me to come, and I'd follow up in a few days by an uninquisitive telephone call that carried affection. I'd let her know I'd be regularly available to help in any way. For I remember that much fuss before the funeral and complete neglect afterward was cruel. Later, I'd try to help her make new contacts and I'd listen with pleasure to any new constructive steps. Above all I'd never use platitudes or meaningless reassurances such as "Be brave," "Try to forget," "You're not the only one." The person in pain is driven to fury by such sentiments.

Very difficult to do, such supporting in friendship, but it's one of the finer ways in which one woman can help another, and if we are rejected we will have at least tried, and the other will know we've tried.

I know that as I age I have to find new friends, preferably younger, as the old ones die off. I'm diminished by each death, whether family or acquaintance. Yet somehow don't I feel safer for the fact that *I* have survived? We can't repine and cry out our loneliness, "No one left!" I've seen those who do. And in old age one grows (of necessity) less emotionally involved with people and issues, less stirred by their virtues but with more tolerance (one hopes) for their faults. For in the making of friends, like tends to seek like, because it's safer with a new person to have common ground on which to plant our feet.

Yet friendships, intimate ones, have been rare with me. I have many friends, but with how many do I deeply share? Was it from family example or tendency to isolation and privacy? My great-great-grandmother, by hearsay and letters, had but one really close woman friend, outside of family members. Grandmother had only one, a first cousin. Mother had two permanent ones, to my knowledge, ones she entrusted with a little of herself: a college roommate, seldom seen, and a second cousin. As for myself, because I had none except cousins when young or in the early years of college (my last year was better), and because Alec and children did not permit the time to make women friends, even had I known how, I never realized what it was to laugh and talk and share and go tootling off anywhere or to the movies or to lunch. I couldn't thoroughly relax. I watched what I said. It was better in a way with my peers at work, but that was shop talk. Dedication, deadly serious dedication to duty and no play was my upbringing with the ingraining of "pay your way" as a password. You never could let up and laugh and sit loose to life.

Could I not now see the beginnings of that delicate, almost intangible, rapport between two women that holds a quality of tenderness and respect and sensitivity to needs, and very deep quiet love? We could talk on the peeling of eggs, on propagating a plant, or deep hurt and anger, or on a better place to buy fresh fish, or walk together to watch the sudden bursting out of lady's slippers, or sit and discuss ideas and ideals, all part of one flow that we have learned has not and never will be betrayed.

People with whom I am not necessarily intimate tend to share with me (the social worker label sometimes opens doors), and one friend, not seen for a long time, told me openly and joyously of her grand passion. Though she was over seventy, her love affair was so intense, so exquisite in its complete and passionate surrender of mind and body to a sexuality never experienced before, that she seemed transfixed. I envied her. It seemed so right, so beautiful.

Even if we as children have been taught about sex comfortably, even if our own marriage relationships have been lusty and healthy and joyful, old age seems somehow to find many of us closing mental doors on our naturalness in this area. And we feel guilt and shame and instinctively repress and tend to hide any signs of affection, perhaps even giving up holding hands with our mate (in public at least)—an innocent bond that is so pleasant.

There is one startling blind spot in society's overall view of the aged: it is the possibility of the existence of a need for continued sexual activity (or substitutes for it). Consider the blatant blindness in the custom of separating couples who enter nursing homes together, or one soon after the other. There is enough fear entailed, enough anxiety aroused, to magnify the cruelty of deliberate deprivation of the opportunity to cling, comfort, reassure, lie close together in one bed, or at least one room. Two lonely individuals on Social Security can often live more inexpensively and happily if they do not marry but share the same quarters. If the young can do it, why not the old? Why not change the Social Security rules so that marrying would no longer be financially punishable?

But I knew why we had blinders on when it came to sex among the elderly. I knew it from my profession and from the voice within me to which I was now listening. I had known what it was to stand outside a parent's closed door. I knew how I felt when Alec and I were first in love and I was told that marital relations were strictly a matter of duty—that the woman was the servant of the male in this area, and that one must never, never withhold sex, either for gain or as punishment—and I was furious that a thing so beautiful as our love should be spoiled or tainted by the thought of middle-aged people having sex. And I knew when middle-aged myself, and my parents in their late seventies, that any idea of sex between them was intolerable. I always put it out of my mind.

And if they had been widowed and married again, it must be without sex. For the father, a housekeeper-mother-nurse kind of wife, who has plenty of money of her own, who covets none of the family possessions or assets, and who is long beyond the child-bearing age. Of course she must be totally asexual. For the mother, a strong, still healthy, rich man who would relieve her loneliness and do all the odd jobs previously done by the children, relieving them of their concern for her. A marriage of convenience. A marriage without sex.

Yes, I could understand the general reaction of society to erotic pleasure among the old. And yet I clung to the beauty of my friend's face as she described her affair, and I clung to the remark made by Princess Marie Bonaparte, a Freudian analyst, who was in her eighties when asked at what age a woman's sexual activity ceases. She is said to have answered, "I don't know. I'm not old enough yet."

I wonder what it will be like for today's young people when they reach their seventies and eighties. For most of them, sex involves few taboos—and the intact hymen holds no charm. They unite bodily in noncommittal, non-binding relationships as easily as they seem to separate when the attraction fades. Some of them, of course, believe that such cohabitation is preparing them more fully for an understanding and compatible married life. They may indeed be better off than we who tended to rush into marriage when overcome with a passion that was partly unfulfilled sexual need, and partly an overidealization, a projection of our romantic dreams onto the loved ones. We, unlike the young of today, had no way of knowing what the day-to-day realities of cohabitation would do to our love. Will these young lovers enjoy or be permitted to enjoy their sexuality when they grow old? Will we have broken down the taboos against "geriatric" sex by that time, as we have broken through the shame of the word *cancer?* If their early sexual freedom does not fail them, the young have a fair chance of experiencing greater richness later on.

After Alec died I found it difficult for some time to smile at any man, to let my face brighten with interest, since in fact I had no interest in him whatever. But I am changing. The little lure in woman's clothes, stance, eyes, smile—so much an appealing and attractive part of the younger personality—is ours by right also. We are too sensitive to overdo it. My former feeling that "I'm too old for lipstick" has given way to a desire to please the sight of others as well as myself. No one has yet accused me of being a man-chaser, but that would be amusing too.

My own answer to the conflicts we face in our sexuality is to let go—to peel off the layers of conformity. As we become more free in general, with age, let us dare to be relaxed in the sexual area also. (We are hardly likely to become promiscuous, after all.) The quality of our physical loving may be different, with less lust and far more tenderness and thoughtfulness—and perhaps timidity—than when we were younger. Touch, closeness, caresses, gentle massage, lying in contact or holding hands are very important substitutes for the sexual act. When we love, we do not see our mates as the young view us—wrinkled, misshapen, unattractive. We still retain, somewhere, the memory of one another as beautiful and lustful, and we see each other at our once-best. But now there is added the spiritual richness from years of patience, familiarity, and fusion of self-in-another. Our fantasies may run in any direction we choose and the touch becomes sweet to us, the warm familiar body smell a fragrance, and we slip into a peace of stillness and relaxation and safety. We can at least dream directly of sexual desire and fulfillment; even if in the process our mother is chasing us, about to destroy us, and we wake (as I did once) just before she catches us, wake to safety, fullness, and desire and that indescribable body delight.

For sensual body response, whether sex is completed or not, is part of the beauty of our narrowing lives.

CHAPTER 16

Before I left the Pain Unit one of the instructors suggested I go at some point to the Insight Meditation Society Retreat, which she herself attended as often as she could. She felt I was ready for what it offered, but suggested one week might be enough for a first time. In late February I received my brochure. We would rise at four-thirty every morning (ugh); we would be two to a room and sleep on foam rubber on the floor (ugh); we would do sitting meditation, walking meditation, eating meditation alternately all day until nine-thirty at night (what?), with the exception of an hour after lunch (thank God for that); all food was vegetarian with just tea and fruit for supper (ugh); and silence was maintained at all times (ah!). No alcohol, of course (ugh). I decided to dare to dare again and signed up for a week in March. Was there something more I needed to learn, to understand? Why else was I still searching?

I had been feeling quietly sad, namelessly sad, for some days at this time, and I realized now I had at last done some deep grieving for Mother. I thought of the well on our old farm, that circular stone well with a great round wooden cover and a small square opening with a lid in the middle. And I lifted the lid and looked down as I used to at the faraway, dark yet sharp reflections of my head and shoulders and the trees above me, and changing focus I saw my old green frog sitting on the projection of a stone, and then Mother's reflection joined mine, and we both, as in my childhood, studied the limpid, pure, motionless water, and she dropped a pebble down and we watched the frog jump and the small ripplets rebound back from the walls in crazy patterns until we could see our absolutely clear duplications imposed there together once again.

I had thought through Mother in the past year, and thought Mother through now, grieving and sad in the loss of her and of that lost innocence and simplicity of childhood. Mother was not a lodestar in the sky that I must follow her in her ways. We had danced a dance of guilt, together, in collusion. She had died of it, let herself die, so burdened with a never understood, never relieved load. And now she was a reflection deep within a well, that was all. And all my longing and grief poured out, any anger and resentment forever gone, seeing and feeling only the sweetness of her presence. A lovely lady. *Requiescat in pace*.

And now I looked into that well alone, no longer divided. Could I not at last be free of eternal questioning—the child's "Why the wind?" Then the "Who am I?" Then "Whither going?" then off on a search carrying me deeper and deeper into a busy analytic mental "I." I felt now that the past cannot serve the present. It only distorts it. Could I not at last simply move and have my being, a being without an ego or a never-ending "I," one that runs smoothly on automatic drive? I would try.

And so I went forth to the Insight Meditation Center, quite ignorant of what lay ahead, innocent and open, yet carried along by an instinct that there was something there for me to experience.

Though I was merely going to the middle of the state, it seemed a venture into an unknown wilderness of some danger, the farthest I had driven in several decades. I felt I should carry a gun and lock the car doors. Moreover, it was pouring rain almost the entire way, and I misrouted myself several times because I couldn't read the signs. The road became more and more narrow, with many little hills and valleys, but I found the town of Barre on a hillside, found the right street, found the retreat: by asking.

I discovered later that the great brick building with its huge white columns had once been the main house of a large private estate, with a ballroom in addition to many sitting and bed and bath rooms. The servants' quarters were extensive. Two tennis courts (now the parking lot), a filled-in swimming pool, a two-car garage, and, later, I found, somewhat out of sight, stalls for six more cars. As I looked west to the foothills of the Berkshires, I saw that the view must once have been breathtaking before the trees had become so large. At some point the Catholic Church had bought the place and turned it into a seminary, building a wing of red brick to match, which made a pleasant U-shape, using the ballroom as a chapel, I gather, and adding a large dining room flush with the kitchen area. Then in a later enlargement, an annex was joined to the ell, and a big chapel was erected.

After registration I was shown into the chapel, now the meditation hall (shoes off before entering). It was a beautiful room with large unadorned windows, walls and trim in rich wood in a very subdued design that was quieting to the eye, with a raised carpeted dais at one end in a half alcove that held an equally subdued altar where sat a bronze Buddha. The floor had many individual mats with cushions, and there were a few straight chairs in the back. Some cross-legged students (we were called yogis) were quietly meditating. I picked out a mat in the second row so I would be able to hear the leaders on the dais, and I placed my cushions there.

Next I was shown my room, which was cell-like and up a very steep pair of back stairs, more suitable for novices or young meditators than for an octogenarian. The room contained in toto one straight folding chair and one iron bedstead with a thin foam-rubber mattress on plywood. I was lucky; they must have taken one look at me and decided to give me one of the few bedsteads in the entire place. When I rise from the floor, I rise awkwardly—like a camel, rear first. Fortunately the place wasn't full, as we were a group of only eighty, so I was assigned no roommate. There was one window, a closet with shelves and a sink. Down the hall were showers and toilets. A sign on my basin requested the occupant not to use the hot water tap. "The faucet will be fixed as soon as may be. Metta." That quaint equivoque reverberated happily in my mind the entire week I was there. The meditator lives in the present. In due course things happen, maybe.

The dining room was huge with long tables holding eight, ten, or twelve. Two other tables held identical arrays of food, and before these, in long silent rows, we moved patiently to get our meal. (My daily job was to wash with soap and water every table after the noon meal. It filled my one-hour rest period, alas.) No paper napkins. Each of us had picked, out of a stack, one soup plate, one dinner plate, a mug, and utensils. These we washed individually in the double-sink pantry, dried on bath towels that were fresh daily, and returned them to our particular chosen spot where we could find them for the next meal.

It was not simply tea and fruit that night, since everyone had been traveling to get there, but a "hearty" meal consisting of grainy homemade bread, margarine, a thick vegetable soup, and several herb teas. I found it very, very satisfactory. At table everyone talked softly, and returnees showed quiet delight at seeing one another again.

Then we all went to the meditation hall, leaving our shoes in neat rows in an anteroom that was also the coat-room, and carrying in our blankets or jackets for our shoulders. The whole place, to my old bones, was consistently and continuously cold. This helped to explain the phenomenally low cost per day that I had noted in the brochure. Every vegetable peeling was saved for soup and finally went into the mulch pile. Every conceivable economy was used. All leaders gave their time free. The mortgage was a high one and many repairs on the buildings were needed. But I noticed with interest that the total of all staff stipend and benefits that year were $7,755.00.

I wasted time the first few days in being watchful and evaluative in this alien atmosphere. I knew nothing about Vipanassa meditation, or retreats, or silence.

Then I suddenly capitulated from the suspicious old woman to the accepting and trusting child, and things improved. I stopped trying to sit precisely as the others did, took a soft beach chair I had brought, put a cushion to keep my low back bent and curved, stuck my feet out in front of me, wrapped my blankets around me, and went to work.

That first evening after supper as we gathered for meditation we were given the general rules. There would be complete silence except in conference with a teacher or in the question period after one of the evening talks, and no reading, writing, drinking, or sex (smoking was permitted outdoors). Responsibilities had already been outlined; everyone had his job. There seemed to be little need to emphasize a sense of responsibility among those serious, high-minded, and earnest people. I had no occasion to change that opinion later.

I lack the mentality to give an idea of the practice of Insight Meditation in any rational way. There was too much as yet to learn. But I got certain gut feelings about it; that I should sit as erect as I could, alert yet relaxed; that I should focus on my breathing, so essentially a part of my being and so available to conscious awareness. By concentrating on my breath, constantly aware of the "rising, falling" of my midriff and abdomen (diaphragmatic breathing), I worked to quiet my thinking, and since that was impossible for me (and for most people), I learned to capture sensations and thoughts as they came, and label them, name the place my mind had gone rushing off to. So, for instance, sitting there, I get an itch. Itches come in the oddest places at the oddest moments when meditating. I deliberately focus on the itch and its chosen spot and think "itching, itching" and linger on that spot for a moment. And by God, the itch invariably goes. Then I go back to my breathing again or I find myself running off in a fantasy that gets me very angry. I've already started to enlarge on my hurt feelings. But I focus on the concept "angry, angry," the state of mind I am currently in, and the disk of my rage slows, the needle sticks in the groove, the platter repeats for a moment and stops. I am angry, that's all. I slip back to my awareness of breathing again. The mind is a terrible master but a wonderful servant. Pain was more difficult, I found. I think, "hurting, hurting" and try to flow into the pain and then go back to breathing awareness again, and if it is a minor pain or a cramp, it too goes away. One of the evening talks suggested that there is a certain amount of pain until one gets used to sitting cross-legged and that if pain still continues hours after one has risen and moved around, then probably one should take another posture while sitting. But the general meditation approach to pain seemed to be that one could eventually develop a willingness to be uncomfortable, to allow pain to happen and to release body tension through it. That one could reach out to pain and sit to it, round, soft, accepting all of it in the mind. The pain was part of life's experience; if we allow it to happen we develop the openness of mind to accept what's going on. In other words, pain is extremely useful in achieving concentration in meditation. This was all too much for me at the time. I had to see the process in very simple terms. The comparison that came to my mind was that of a child running to its mother (my mind was the child, I, my person, sitting there, was the parent). So my child comes running and crying, "I fell, it hurts! See!" And I the mother say, "Let me look. Yes, of course it hurts. That's a mean bump." And the child says, "Yes it does," and goes back to its game. Or the child is in a rage at friend Susie, who grabbed her doll and ran with it. She comes to complain to Mother, "I hate Susie. She stole my doll, I hate her!" And the mother says, "Yes, you're angry, I can see that. And now you've told me, why don't you run out and find Susie and go on playing dolls again." The child discovers that with a moment of acceptance and concentration both anger and hurt have gone. And I, sitting there, have found my anger is gone. I begin to see how quick anger can be in me and that I'm afraid of pain, and I learn to go quiet on them.

And as I gradually stilled that buzzing vagabond mind of mine, and calm began to come, I even lost the sensation of having hands or legs, or a body, and then once or twice of even having a me. This happened, but not often. I had a long, long way to go.

I learned how to picture all my mind states, emotions, anxieties, or plans or projections of the future, even memories or miseries of the past, as being simply chemical and electrical activity that need not be my terrible master. And by discipline and long training I could learn to control them, maybe.

This only hinted at the scope of a discipline leading to choiceless awareness and mind-heart integration. But for some, in a certain time of mental stillness there can come enlightenment, a moment of exquisite bliss, that state that the searching Buddha captured as he sat under his bodhi tree. Christianity focused on "The Word" of God. In Buddhism it was "The Way" of Man. And we were taught that the Buddha was no god, but simply a man who had worked out a way, a path, to find simplicity and peace in the pain and storms of life.

One day in the meditation hall my eidetic imagery ran away from its job of breathing, and saw the bronze statue of Buddha up there on the low altar, and then visualized the crucifix that had probably hung there under the aegis of the Church. I thought of Christ on the Cross, suspended above the earth, his tormented body showing his agony in the drawn-up belly, extended ribs and hard veins, the head drooping like a wilted flower on the chest, in death, and the whole figure representing the suffering of mankind and the cruelty of man to man. Yet that same artifact stood for sacrifice and love and forgiveness and resurrection. The Buddha, on the other hand, sat in the lotus position, body planted firmly and fused into the earth, robes folded softly and evenly about him, slant eyes half closed, face calm, lips sometimes parted in a quarter-smile, big belly relaxed and full of benison as was his whole body. A symbol of loving-kindness. And the two symbols would neither fuse nor superimpose.

In a way the early mornings were the best. It was still night when the first sound of the gong woke the place. The clarion ring came from a heavy Burmese brass triangle, and its reverberations were clear and pure and long lasting as they carried through the halls and faded into the distance. Then came quick dressing and going to slip into the meditation hall wrapped in blankets, to sit quietly, to sink into an inner stillness as other figures settled themselves around. Now my mind would generally quiet to a few passing random thoughts and then to an utter peaceful silence.

A single little touch on a small gong signaled the end of the hour. Dawn was coming in through the windows. Each time it seemed to me like a curious new awakening for myself.

In walking meditation one could walk fast or could take infinitely slow steps. I wobbled if I did the latter. Every muscle was concentrated on, every slight tension noted. If thoughts wandered, you brought them quietly back by concentrating on lift, forward, step.

At first, as I moved evenly back and forth in the old ballroom, surrounded by those other slow-moving figures with their unresponsive eyes, it seemed to me that they fitted into a once recurring dream of mine: I saw them on a dimly lighted stage, flowing rhythmically, even-paced, crisscrossing back and forth, and I sensed that they all hated me and at some point they would focus on me, move in, and destroy me. It was during the next sitting meditation that I realized that it was the women who were really bothering me—in spite of the fact that they were all so pleasant looking—and then suddenly it dawned on me that they were all one, an angry and disapproving mother figure who would not look at me because I had been bad. And with that recognition I almost laughed, ceased to have any concern and was able to float slowly in silence among the others.

This was a place where I never needed to smile politely or say pleasant words. I don't know what it was like for others, for I never talked with anyone about it. But for me, God! That freedom was beautiful!

Eating meditation was a continuation of the others. Not only was the food delicious, well seasoned, with new textures and tastes, but my appetite was enormous from all that mental nonwork. We tended to sit apart, all looking out the window, at a wall, or in total unfocus. I kept my thoughts on the motions of my tongue, the act of swallowing, the contact of the teeth together, the textures of food, the motion of my hand carrying the spoon from plate to mouth. Every gesture was noted, every motion made slowly and in full rumination. My mind leapt back to the rumen of the cow eating grass.

The last meal of the day was at 5:30 and usually consisted of peanuts, an apple, and herb tea, several kinds. Often there was vegetable broth at 9:30 before bed, and I had brought a secret cache of Granola Bars in case I got too hungry. I never knew how kind such light food could be to the body, and for a few days after the retreat (the first night back I indulged myself with bourbon, steak, and fried onions), I experienced considerable indigestion.

I said good-bye to no one, for silence still

held us, and all the others were continuing the second week. But one pretty young girl saw me in the hall and whispered, "You're not going?" When I nodded, tears came to her eyes and she quickly threw her arms around me and then ran. What was that all about? Our eyes had never met, although I had often noticed her in the dining room when I was cleaning the tables.

I was leaving too soon. I had only begun. I had had a first taste of mental stillness, body stillness, of low soft breathing, of a totality that did not need to feel tension to move, and I heard the whisper of the sense of nonbeing while still being. As I drove through and over the hills, my mind kept saying, "Go back, go back!" and I knew I would.

At home I at once felt the change. The techniques had carried over into my daily life. Now I walked at a pace in which all of me moved in rhythm and there was a sense of repetitive dance within me. Now the times of resting my back were more than a deliberate relaxation of muscles. They were a quieting of mind, often to a stillness that held great depth. Now things got done so easily that I neither anticipated nor reminded myself, and activity, whether for coming company or writing, was so effortless I seemed to float. My self-consciousness had gone.

I returned to yoga classes and learned the breathing techniques—empty the lungs with the peaking of every physical effort, then inspire quickly again. My daily exercises became synchronized, flowing and fully pleasurable. They were another little island of quiet mindless time.

And sometimes I felt as if I were sitting under my own mental bodhi tree, learning the truth of egolessness, and that this was the state of man in his innocence before the Fall.

CHAPTER 17

Now I was in springtime again. An allegory for my journey came to mind from a childhood story book of Noah, the Ark, and the floods, with each step of the great and awful and simple tale so graphically and delicately illustrated. I can see once more the arduous labor of building the great clumsy closed ship on the level plain, a ship without rudder or sail, built of necessity as a family enterprise, since all other people scoffed. Then came the slow movement, amid urging and persuasion and force, of all animal life, two by two, male and female, into the Ark, along with enormous supplies of food; the closing of the great door on the side; from without the jeers of the doubters, and within, the waiting, waiting. But finally the rains came, slow at first, heavier and heavier, mightier and mightier, rising swiftly over the land, the Ark finally lifting, floating light and free (I still see the last people clinging uselessly and desperately to mountain peaks), the ship now to be flung and tossed on the raging seas, lightning and storm clouds without, and within, first homesickness, then dreadful seasickness, then complaints, and finally raging fights among species, with Noah, Shem, Ham, and Japheth trying desperately to keep order and control; then calmer waters, and a very soft even floating of the Ark; the dove sent out from the roof opening only to come back soon, having found no place to rest her feet or wings; in another two weeks sent out again, returning with a small olive twig bearing green leaves, and hope leapt in the breast of every beast and man; more weeks, the Ark thumped and bumped and stopped and stuck on a sloping mountainside: the great door was opened, the animals streamed out to slosh and slide and slip in thick clinging mud.

And then the final picture—oh joy! —showing the ground carpeted with flowers, the trees tender in their soft new green, a line of the wildest animals, still two by two, moving off into the distance to find their own places, wild to mate, while in the foreground the smaller animals leapt and gamboled. Particularly did I like the lissome little pink pigs, flowers behind their ears, dancing on their hind legs, and the laughing lambs capering in the sunlight, and all the while Noah looked benignly on. And the great dark Ark, high and askew and aslant on the mountainside, lay empty, to be used nevermore, prey now only to slow rot.

Over all rose the great brilliant rainbow of promise, arching the whole sky. That last picture represented my spring that year of 1980.

Since January, I had been thinking energetically of my beach house. I could, physically and emotionally, now make it a home, my home, and bestow some charm upon it. And through the months I studied every catalogue and every sale at stores and ordered and accumulated many necessary articles. A thing as simple as a vase, last summer, was nonexistent. I had to use an ancient bean pot that lacked a cover, and candles were stuck in empty wine bottles. I spent, how I spent! On myself, on clothes, on my house, for the first time in my life without sharp twinges of guilt and of unworthiness. No, I didn't go overboard, but I had a wonderful time, and in my springtime mood I panted to refurbish my nest.

In June, when the new brochure of the meditation retreat came I signed up for two weeks at the end of September. And I went to the Registry of Motor Vehicles to renew my five-year license, that license I had gotten first in 1916. "Read the third line down," said the woman behind the counter. "Try the second . . . read the top?" No, I couldn't read even the top line. All three were a faint gray blur. "See your oculist," she told me, kindly enough. "You need a new prescription." My ophthalmologist looked anxious, for my right eye had lost ability to focus about ten years before, but I returned to the Registry ten days later with a letter from him and my new glasses. The same woman was there. I still couldn't read the top line, although at least I could see vaguely that there were letters. "No way," she said, still kindly.

I told her that I had never had an accident in sixty-four years of driving, and that I used the car only in a traffic-free country area within a three-mile radius on familiar roads, and that I rarely went out. She looked at the doctor's letter, shook her head at herself. "I have no business," she said,

"I have no business," and handed me my license. "Wear your glasses when you get your picture taken." I went home in sober triumph. How was it that my eyes had changed so dramatically in the ten days since I saw my ophthalmologist? And how, in conscience, could I go on driving?

Grandchildren drove me to the beach, our two cars full, including all my plants, they settled me in, and as days went by took on the task of mending shades, springs, broken locks, moving around ugly furniture in such ways that rooms took on a charm out of sheer inappropriateness. They humored me in my desire to have all kitchen utensils, measuring cups, spoons, knives, pot lids hung in plain sight and handy for use. All this effort seemed to me very important, though I didn't consciously connect it yet with my eyes.

This was a summer to be joyous in freedom. A time to walk again the tufty dusty little paths that led from house to house to tennis court to beach, with only the intent of direction in mind, the rest of me floating in lovely familiarity and the sweet salt smell wafting from the sea.

A time to celebrate the Fourth of July at our favorite picnic spot at the end of the neck (once two islands); the route to it is perilous for the elderly, over uneven boulders, up a little cliff (which I once used to run up or down lightly), through poison ivy and wild-rose and bayberry and blackberry. At the end of the point is a flat granite ledge, from where only lobster-pot markers can be seen, then a few stray boats, a mournful red bell buoy, and the shoreline curving northeastward to Maine.

It was a clear evening. The air was fresh and salty. There must have been fifty of us, of all ages, mostly relatives, gathered there to celebrate the Fourth. Our little driftwood fires blazed and lovely cooking smells wafted in the air. We drank, we ate, we sang. The harmony of young voices, clear and sweet in the coming dusk, was deeply poignant to me. When the sun set over the low hills across the water, gloriously red, I realized that I had never expected to get out here again.

A temptation almost too great rose in me to do as of yore, when the tide was high—move down to the rim of the black water, drop my clothes from me, and, sitting on the gradual ledge, slide myself down through seaweed into the mysterious water, full of danger and monsters and slimy frightening soft things that could suck you down. Always a bet with myself that I didn't dare. Always I did dare and came out shivering from the deep dark night of the sea.

But I shook my head at myself and my age (I could have done it, though, cautiously), and a grandson escorted me back to the mainland as dark settled in. I drove home. From my porch I heard the singing going on, and clear bursts of laughter. I watched the simple fireworks flash out. When the lights, the voices, the pops and bangs had all died away and the island fires had faded into darkness, I went easily to bed. Could there be greater happiness than this?

That summer was a time for becoming acquainted with my one-year-old great-granddaughter—and for marveling once more at the wonder of heredity. Thomas Hardy said it for me: "I am the family face; / Flesh perishes, I live on, / Projecting trait and trace / Through time to times anon. . . . The eternal thing in man, / That heeds no call to die."

It was a time to row again, for the first time since my accident some twenty years before. The oars clicked evenly between the tholepins. My stroke was still steady and—yes—strong. I feathered the oars with the old familiar wrist-bend, and with deep joy felt my back lean into the motion. I, my boat and I, alone, moving swift and free.

A time to make a collection of horseshoe-crab shells. I decided to make a great circle of them on a bare porch wall, each crab treading on the long tail of the one before. There is always a crop of little cousins (much removed) at the beach, of horseshoe-crab-gathering ages. I offered them ten cents for every crabshell they discovered in the wrack from winter storms; but I stipulated that each must be a slightly different size or shape from those I already had. And I offered a bonus for the tiny, almost translucent cream-colored baby carapaces, the same tone as the dead straw in which they are found. A very shy little cousin with big eyes came alone, offered his crab timidly, and fled. Two agile little girls danced in and, clutching their dimes, swung in my hammock and talked to each other. I ended the summer with nineteen crabs ranging in size from two to fourteen inches. I plan to send the young gathering again another year.

It was a time to outline the calloused,

spread-toed bare feet of those children on pieces of paper. (My pen tickled them.) Next year I would cut these out and paste them on new, larger foot-outlines; and again the next year and the next, as long as may be. Better, in a way, for understanding growth than the height mark on a closet door.

A time to lie on the beach and feel the warm sand under my cheek; to turn a shell over and over with an idle hand, or to make smoothing or roughing motions with it; to let my body soak up sun until it became imperative to plunge into the shocking water. How long had it been since I had utterly let loose that way?

A time to gather mussels at extra-low, full-moon ebb tides. I was on the beach by five-thirty one morning, carrying two plastic bags. And as I had done as a child, so now I wondered at the utter stillness, the clarity, the limpid water where even shadows of boats seemed asleep, the cove wrapped in its own isolation. I tore the tightly wedged mussels from their rocks and trudged up the cliff path as the tide crept in over the sand and shell beds. There were to be moules marinière for the company that night—until I found out that the mussels in this area were temporarily toxic from "red tide" and unfit to eat. How silly! I lugged them all the way down to the beach again, hoping they would be able to reattach themselves to the rocks. A cosmic question that I did not dwell upon for long.

This was a time for my distant children and grandchildren to visit, together or separately. They entered into my joy in reorganizing the house, and wallpapered and cleaned and cooked and shopped. And the time came, quite without forethought, when I heard myself saying perfectly comfortably to a grown granddaughter and her boyfriend, "Do you want the room with the double bed, or twin beds, or separate rooms?"

A time to take all available granddaughters on a spending spree (not all at once) to buy each an outfit she could not otherwise afford. They looked so well in almost anything, with their fine long-legged slimness, and the differences in taste fascinated me. Strong personalities already. It was a treat for us all, with closeness, with fun.

This was *not* a time for a food processor to malfunction, but such was the case. Slicing beans for a late supper, I discovered that the motor hadn't turned off as it should when I took off the cover. The slicing disk appeared motionless and I started to remove it. It was rotating, in fact, at a speed too high for my sight; and the balls of the first two fingers on my right hand were nicely and neatly sliced off. Curiously, I registered only mild and resigned concern. Pressing my fingers hard against a wad of Kleenex in my palm, I called a grandchild for help.

The hospital emergency room was dark and empty that terribly hot and steamy night. A nurse sat in a little lighted cubicle waiting for stupid people like me. Lights blazed on; my fingers were examined several times before a plastic surgeon arrived from his home. Yes, he had finished his dinner, he told me when I asked him apologetically. My grandson sat quietly in a corner. This was my chance of a lifetime to see at arm's length how skin grafts are done. It was a beautiful though tedious job. My forearm was the donor. My only criticism was—and I had to control my urge to tell him—that the doctor used too long a wire for sewing, his arm extending way out with each stitch. A short thread is always more efficient.

Thinking of my own delayed supper, I asked the nurse if they had hot dogs in the hospital coffee shop. The doctor grunted his amusement. "You'll be dizzy and nauseated when we're through. You'll go straight home and to bed." I almost said, "What'll you bet?"—but decided not to distract him. Soon it was done, the forearm in a cast. The cast in a sling. I sat up. No dizziness, no nausea, only good honest hunger. But by the time I had had tetanus shots ("One in yer arm, one in yer bum," the bright little nurse said) and got my three Percodan pills for the night, the coffee shop was closed. I asked my grandson to drive me to a hot dog stand. Never did filet mignon taste so good.

Back in my kitchen again, my grandson, opening a beer for me, asked what he should do with the beans still in the processor. I suggested we might rinse them clean. He looked in the container, grimaced, and shoved it under my nose. We threw the beans outside for the nightly raccoons. Their sensitive agile little paws are so selective.

Lying in bed, my arm out of its sling and high on pillows, alone in the house again, sipping my beer, novocaine wearing off and Percodan swallowed, I still wished I had made that bet with the doctor. In the morning I found my left hand to be even more uncoordinated than I had always known it was. My toothbrush jerked and jumped in my mouth, never hitting where it should. But I managed a tub bath—getting out only after quite a few tries—and I made breakfast and my bed, all with one hand, too.

And it was a time to celebrate an eightieth birthday: my own; the eightieth, with its connotations, the most significant of all birthday decades.

I look back now. That summer day was a rarity, neither too hot nor too cold, too windy nor too calm, too sunny nor too gray. A soft little breeze drew in off the water. For an occasion like this, no caterers: my female progeny produced gourmet hors d'oeuvres, hot and cold, and the eleven young and lissome granddaughters passed them around, the six grandsons and sons-in-law tending bar. The presents, again, were in family style (jars of jelly, plants, wild or garden flower bouquets, fruit, poems and a bottle of perfume); and from my children a group photograph to be taken—every last member there, from far and near, and even the photographer a great-nephew on his way to becoming a professional. Above all, no hints, before or later, of dissension or discord anywhere among so many descendants. Instead, a sense of euphony emanating from them as a group working as one. The seventy or more guests were largely relatives; and here too a noticeable quality, almost a resonance of happy feeling, prevailed. People seemed to be bonded together in great good fellowship—a renewing of acquaintances, a mending of fences—everyone warm, outgoing, almost a self-appointed greeter to everyone else—a flow of vicarious exultation.

And then the speeches, and my discomfort and gratification began. Spontaneously one person after another mounted the porch steps and stood beside me (while I clung to a post), saying moving, loving, funny, reminiscent, laudatory, intense, even painful, even beautiful words. And as it went on and on a sort of fugue came over me, a crazy feeling that I had returned from the dead to listen to my own eulogies. For my friends spoke almost as if they were afraid they were going to lose me; or even, almost, as if they had already lost me.

The party continued into the small hours, long after I had tucked in for the night. What an altogether and infinitely soul-satisfying party! What an out-of-this-world birthday celebration! Love! For once all love, and I could accept it happily.

CHAPTER 18

Finally there was the summer's ending. Labor Day was once again upon us all. I sat on my upper porch late, late that night. Out there before me the cove, the dark-lying neck, the sea beyond, and miles away on the Ipswich and Newburyport shores and up into New Hampshire lay the necklace of lights of small communities of men. Utterly clear, warm, and still. I sat waiting, feet up, and floating. . . .

A memory came sharp. Now I was a little girl, four or five, at last allowed on the beach alone, and I had gone down there early, for it was full-moon low tide, and there in the corner of the sand by the island lay lots of rounded stones that held beneath them baby crabs and the flat many-legged squiggly worms that stirred in the sandy muck when I shifted or lifted a rock to expose them to light. But one, too heavy for me, dropped back into its ooze which splashed up and dirtied my last clean dress. I was bad again! I straightened up and looked across that seemingly vast stretch of sand, those high granite ledges, out to the limitless sea. I saw nothing but enormity. I suddenly knew, for the first time ever, that I was an I, a little girl in a dirty white dress, and I looked at me and saw that I was there, alone, on the wide beach, very small and very big at the same moment. I had *found* a little Harriet!

Was there a special meaning in this small bit of unspoiled coastline that held me so tightly within its arms? I waited there in the dark, floating again. . . . I was back in a biology class in high school, and life opened before me. "Ontogeny recapitulates phylogeny," words meaningless to my undeveloped brain, but so full of intensity in my visceral responses. For I had been the bit of amino acid, the speck of protoplasm, the single amoebalike cell with its nucleus, now punctured by another cell, a spermatozoon; next many cells dividing with incredible speed, not as a cancer proliferates, but each with a specific drive to develop, within a few days, gills for drawing oxygen from water, fins, to form flippers for hauling and crawling on drying land, then rudimentary arms, even a semblance of a tail in a recapitulation of the whole history of the development of life. And the fluid in which every cell of my body was bathed contained salt of much the same density as the sea lying out there before me at this moment.

I wanted to sit on the high smooth ledge above the pier. Without lights I went carefully downstairs, off the lower porch, and walked out to sit on the rounded, lichened rock, rubbed down by glaciers. From here I could see the blinking light of the Isles of Shoals off the Maine coast. A wondering came strong now. Was it because I was born here and the first breath I drew was salt-tinged, or because I first discovered "Harriet" here, or because in my lonely childhood exploring I knew the littoral scene so intimately, knew the changes year by year when, returning each spring, I covered every inch of the shoreline, noting how the beach had eroded or the sand thrust up or how rock had been exposed, how fissures had widened in granite, how the great quarried stones of our boat pier moved slightly from winter storms that lifted and shifted the granite as it was lightened by its great flukes of ice. And adding gradually to those childhood discoverings, I learned that under that ocean there had once been dry land, dry for a hundred miles out during a glacial period (had I not discovered one summer at full neap tide a great bed of disintegrating toppled spruce trees that grew only in a far colder climate—a little forest from which all sand had been sucked by a bad winter storm?). And I learned that, through the motion of continents, that little space of shore was lifted each century by a few inches, and was pushed farther away from Europe by great forces within the earth, and that those billions of tiny white barnacles, moving with infinite slowness to another little space, there to feed on a different bit of effluent or fleet float, scraped away at the rocks and eroded them year by year? This place was a microcosm, and was I not, at every moment while there, aware inside of the changes in the tides, reacting emotionally to the phases of the moon—that moon that dies so faintly silver white in the sky to a nothing and then is reborn again, fully, in another twenty-eight days just as my own adolescent cycle repeated faithfully the moon's timing? And among the wrack, the flotsam and jetsam above high tide, every crab carapace, every limpet shell, brittle sea anemone, bit of driftwood, seed pod, dried straw of march grass each had had its own destiny as I had mine.

This ledge was always my ponder-place as a child, as young adult, as middle-aged matron, and now as that simpleminded and sentimental old woman. It was such a hot still night for the end of August, no radiational cooling but only a fresh little breath from the water, that the midges began nipping and the few mosquitoes droned and lit. But I must consider the night sky first. I had done so often enough in the years past, particularly at midnight on the full moon tides when the land seemed to lift and float.

That very afternoon, there on the same ledge where I had a wide view of a clear and windless blue ether, I watched as a jet, far too high for me to see, left its long white vapor trail, sharp and distinct. In a minute another jet, then another, then another. Some military maneuvers perhaps. Yet each white trail lay farther west than the preceding one so that there were parallel lines of white in the sky. I wondered why they flew miles apart instead of following one another. Not so, said someone later at cocktails, for he too had observed the phenomenon. They *are* following each other exactly, but we are running away from *them,* since we're rotating so rapidly with the earth. Oh! And now in my whole body I felt the earth's flight for the first time and sensed the speed of our revolutions in space. Like other stars, other planets, each set in its immemorial order.

Yet behind the calm of the night sky (ah! another shooting star going into nowhere) existed such awful force and violence, such repelling and attracting of gravitational forces, winds of such incredible speeds around the planets, dust storms of impenetrable density, incomprehensible cold, incomprehensible heat, explosions, meteors flying off to perhaps in-thrust somewhere, or explosions of such intensity that there was nothing but innerness, never to emerge again from the sucking black holes. All this around those planets and stars and galaxies all being pulled by gravity or flying away forever to nowhere. Such violence within such calm peace. And here below such violence within each poor puny suffering little human. . . .

Man's foetal vestigial gills quickly sloughed off or were absorbed, but his primitive brain with the response to danger of fight/flight, so vital to the original survival of the species, was still with him with the all too capable adrenal glands pouring out chemical and electrical messages all over the body.

Yet we live in a world that seldom presents a danger that calls for true fight or flight response. Atavistic, yet there the instincts irrevocably are, no longer functional. So our rage and our other emotions, if controlled to meet the demands of the codes of civilization, affect the guts, the heart, the arteries, breathing, and circulation (and the low back!). Hate creates immobility. Grief, if repressed, affects the immune system, leading to illnesses and diseases including cancer. Yet unrepressed grief can feed on itself, as man indeed feeds on himself, and Niobe, whose tears never ceased, had to be turned to stone. And if all emotions are totally repressed, the ending is inanity.

Yet this same man caught in suffering out of his inheritance, wrung and wrought upon by emotions, has the ability to endure, to surmount, create, survive against great odds, and love into the bargain. And he makes his myths to bring light and order out of his emotions. Thus are created our religions and our beliefs and our rites and our rituals and our wars and even our inventions.

And now I was back in reality again. My feet bare and light on the path, I returned to the dark and empty house, up the stairs to my porch. The huge old apple tree, under which I had swung as soon as I could hold on, had not come to leaf this spring. Last year there were only tiny shoots at the tips. I studied its tortured shape against the night sky, beautiful in its storm-bent un-grace, its patient Oriental acceptance of a century. I did not want it chopped down, yet.

I said goodnight to the old apple tree—what fragrant firewood and fine white ash it would make eventually—and to the sea and the horizon and to a last shooting star and to the stillness that lay around and above me, and went to bed.

As I turned out the light I could hear my father's quiet voice quoting one of his many New England maxims, "Never trouble trouble till trouble troubles you."

CHAPTER 19

Reaching home comfortably thanks to the loving care of grandchildren, the beach house to be eventually tucked in for the winter night by my oldest son, everything now unpacked, food supplies in, writing materials waiting, I felt anxiety rise in spite of myself, in spite of breathing relaxation and meditation periods.

The thoughts I had simply not let come to my conscious mind all summer now flooded me. Yes, I had run over curbs when turning corners; yes, I had gone up one-way streets; yes, I had finally limited my driving only to a small mall that contained the few shops necessary to me and went there only by isolated roads at the noon hour; yes—and now I looked back—I had been wiping my glasses clean ever since Christmas, wiping them over and over since they seemed dirty;

yes, in March I had bought several new lamps with very high wattage and in April had canceled both newspapers, feeling that they took too much time from my work; and yes, gradually, plugging along with the book, I began writing double-space with a felt-tip pen the material that I then dictated to my recording machine; and yes, all summer I had done no reading whatever: book or magazine or paper.

"Quick, Grandma! See that boat out there. It's capsized!"

"No, I can't see that boat out there. Tell me about it."

"Here are my pictures from the party. Look!"

"I can tell the larger single faces—explain to me who some of the others are."

That first week in September the "old age" minibus took me to the city for my long-awaited eye appointment. About ten years before, my right eye had lost vision to macular degeneration, that condition where the center of the retina loses ability to register an image. With that right eye I could see light and had peripheral vision of wavy, distorted, dim lines but I saw only darkness when I looked directly at something. I knew at that time there was absolutely no cure. "Is my good eye going the same way?" I asked. I had been terrified of this ever since the other eye failed me.

"Yes, I'm sorry, this is it. We'll have to wait and see how far the degeneration goes. I'll be seeing you every six weeks. Do you mind if I telephone your son?" Why the hell did he want to talk with my son? Why not with me? Oh, we were both so very matter-of-fact. The doctor gave me no advice, no suggestions, merely two large magnifying glasses on bases to try out. I knew he cared. He is a nice man, and his pacing of the room was a cover for his sympathy. I had a feeling he was waiting for me to begin crying.

About an hour after I reached home, while I was still in shock, blankly thinking, "blindness, legal blindness," two cocktail guests, widows, arrived. I was not yet ready to mention my doom to anyone; but I was aware of exactly the same sensation I had felt at that first party I attended after Alec's death; the conversation so inanely cheery, utterly boring, and my having a sense of being incorporeal. I realized at once it was a reaction of grief.

I can't remember how and when I told my children or if I told anybody else. Whatever

I said was without self-indulgence. For everything was put aside in my need to finish this book before I departed for the meditation retreat the end of the month. And my mind was completely split: since I'd blocked off, temporarily, all emotions about myself, how could I "feel" my way into my writing, or flow it out freely?

But I did it, the whole manuscript finished at last. I engaged a driver to take me in my car to the retreat, I sent to my agent the last chapters, and, finally, everything packed and in order, I coldly locked the door and left, taking my delicate hand of Buddha with me. Ostensibly I wanted to ask the implication of the twelve-pointed star in the palm, perhaps the approximate date or branch of Buddhism. But far more. I wanted it with me. I would caress its bronze silkiness in my bad hours. No fetish this, simply a friend and a symbol of man trying to help man endure his pain.

On the way out I told my driver about my eyes, a crack opening in my silence. He thought it was awful not to be able to drive anymore. We reached the great brick house and it looked so solid, so welcoming, so—I had the feeling—unchanging in its habits and its tenets and its honesty. When I registered, warmly welcomed, I told about my eyes and said I would not be able to read notices on the great bulletin board (used for all communications between staff and meditators) and could they type out in capitals the daily schedule for me to keep with me, and also put any conference times for me in individual notes with "Robey" in large dark letters and pin them to the bottom left of the board. They certainly would.

The place was full up this time, about 120 of us yogis, some eighty to stay for the three months' retreat (could I do that? No!), the rest of us for the two weeks. I would have a roommate. Oh, dear! I asked, "Then please give me the last female to arrive," and that last female never did turn up. I had my privacy.

In the first meditation sitting that night I itched and my muscles jerked and my breathing would not loosen or quiet down, and concentration on anything was utterly lacking, my brain still locked. The gong the next morning at four-thirty held sad resonance. And as I sat myself at my place in the meditation hall, I knew from sudden tears in my eyes that a door was trying to open. Again I found no ability to watch the "rising, falling" of my breathing. I was off on a tremendous fantasy, one of myself sitting, sitting, seeing nothing in clarity, no outlines, only wavy shapes: no driving, no reading, no writing, no dictionaries or my beloved reference books: no poetry, no dial numbers or telephone or cookbooks or directions, fumbling over the simplest cooking, picking up shadows off the floor or putting things on counters so they fell off; no recognizing people until they told me who they were, and then unable to read the feelings or expressions in their faces (how would I like being dependent on others for everything in the outside world? I who still found it so hard to ask); sitting hour after hour, eating myself up, or—or—dumping myself in the nursing home.

Self-pity was so thorough, so exaggerated, I was suddenly amused. And then I could start to work on meditation. But oh—how badly I needed, in that two weeks' silence, someone to shout out to, "I'm losing my eyesight! I'm losing my eyesight! Listen, I'm losing . . ." I was too much the female to be able to keep the trauma to myself. Yet there was that ever-present silence around us all.

In the next walking meditation I went outside, and, closing my good left eye, I walked slowly, I walked fast, and found that, where the ground was even, I could proceed comfortably and straight. Even if the good eye became worse than the bad one, I could walk and have my exercise.

At the next sitting I knew anger, but where there is absolutely no object for anger, except fate, it's hard to sustain that feeling, and it became ridiculous. In this non-speaking atmosphere of strangers I couldn't even find anyone or anything to project anger upon.

All the myths of blindness flooded my mind. With every breath came a silent cry of longing for Alec, his strength and his caring, the help and second sight he would have been for me at home, the arms I could rest in. And for a day or two I grieved secretly, deeply and helplessly, until depression weighted me down with its lack of feeling, weighted me down into a deep dark pool of sadness and immobility and—again—self-pity.

I moved like a zombie and a whisper of amusement rose. How safe one was here! What a wonderful place in which to be depressed. My slow dragging moving, my slow dragging eating, my hand going languidly up to my mouth, my eyelids too heavy to lift, all were a near counterpart of the deliberate walking and eating meditation of most of us. Yes, how safe I was here, with nobody defined to anybody else.

About the third night during the evening talk by one of our leaders, the theme focused on the mind-states, those supra-natural emotions, those feelings that can so distract and distort us from simply being. Insight came in one great rush: "Why bother to grieve? Why bother with self-pity?" And I saw a complete dichotomy in choices. I could do as several other people I knew who had the same eye condition, bemoan and live sad and deprived, or I could shove off from my shoulders that Old Man of the Sea that had just taken position and settled himself upon me, his knees gripping me, shake him off, so sharply he would fall to the ground and become only a shadow of memory.

I was in the clear! Now I could see a fact as a fact. When sadness came, as it would, I thought, particularly at tendered tenderness, I now knew I could allow tears to run freely; or I could, as freely, rage briefly at my ineptness while learning to be controlled and precise in motion, touch, and memory, or when totally frustrated in some endeavor.

What use to belabor a dead horse? As for those times when I was totally empty of activity, and at ground zero, I could relax or meditate into the stillness I had so newly learned, or I could play with my mind and all that lay within, an immense journey, or even just twiddle my thumbs.

Joy rose within me. I was in the clear.

Then I made a bet with myself. (Alec would never bet, even on a surety, even laughingly with me. Though he did get very devilish with a twenty-five-cent bet with his army son-in-law at the annual Harvard-West Point game.) I made a bet with my eyes; if they go all the way into the forever unfocused world, I'll treat myself to a new, unneeded, perfectly exquisite, glamorous, terribly expensive dress and, maybe, a new bottle of Joy perfume. If the eye degeneration stops at a point where I can still pick out letters with high magnification and illumination, I lose, but in either case I've won. Hah! After all, must there not be a shadow to give quality to shape?

The mind, like nature, abhors a vacuum. That two weeks was a many-faceted yet fractured time of silence and slow motion. During meditation and in the nights I planned mentally step by step every change I would make in my house and my life when I reached home. And the list, including what I thought were many ingenious ideas, grew and grew. Concerned that I was failing in my task of learning mind-containment, I discussed the problem with a leader in my individual conference. He felt that under the present conditions I should look directly at my problem, but asked me to keep gently drawing my mind back to the breathing.

Planning to return sometime to complete what I was now neglecting, I tried out the daily activities with my better eye closed, and found that, with a little caution and experience, I could be self-sustaining except in filling the soup bowl or mug with tea or soup. I underfilled, overfilled, but usually poured half in, half out. So if and when I came back, I would simply hold out that bowl to the next in the chow line behind me. In this environment it would be carefully filled, and a quick affection and caring would pass between the two of us, without eyes necessarily meeting.

Typing was going to become a necessity for me. I had once taught myself the touch system, though only up to the top line of symbols, and my hands were so stiff after long disuse and perhaps rheumatism that they were now quite uncontrolled, hitting wrong keys or two or three at once. I had given up typing months ago. Now I worked hard on exercising, and it was painful. Daily my hands grew more limber. Could I ever learn to translate straight from the right brain onto the typewriter? Is it possible? Or could I learn to dictate on tape straight from my rapid thoughts?

I knew now my directions when I got home, and I could do no more planning. I began to meditate well, in quiet alert awareness. Once or twice a curious fantasy came that my hands were so large and strong I could lift pain and guilt and insecurity and shame from all troubled ones. What a crazy omnipotent arrogance! Yet one night, in the last meditation of the day, I felt my hands, without volition, almost in spite of my orders, lifting and spreading with urgency of great force to encompass—encompass what? Becoming self-conscious I pulled them down again. Again, as if in hypnosis, they slowly lifted and spread. I didn't like such phenomena—yet—and finally and sternly stopped myself. But after meditation was over, and the leader sat momentarily on the edge of the dais, answering someone's question, I waited and then asked him what my experience was all about. He said that for some reason tremendous psychic energy was in my hands at this time. I was startled. Such ideas are not within my ken. Was it perhaps because my hands were growing strong from being so strongly exercised? But I stored the incident away for possible reference.

On our next-to-last day before leaving, the silence, by permission, broke, and we thirty or so talked our heads off, though quietly in one room so as not to disturb the three-month meditators. How hungrily speech came forth. How we studied each other's faces. How fascinated we were with the animation we now saw for the first time. We were at once all friends. Later I asked the leader whether, if my eyes had fully degenerated by next year, I could still come back. "Certainly," he said, and added, "Metta."

"Metta?" How dumb can I be? Metta was to me a very powerful unknown female in the establishment. All my bulletin notes were signed Metta, pre-retreat letters had been signed Metta, notices on doors or elsewhere were signed Metta. I had tried, in my few glimpses of the volunteer staff, to figure out which one she was: so omnipresent and active. But there was nobody I could ask because there is no speech. And now—some memory came or something clicked. "Metta" was the word for "loving-kindness."

So, wrapped in the loving-kindness of Buddha, I went home, ready to start blindproofing my house.

CHAPTER 20

On my second day home, getting mail from my box, I chatted with a neighbor I knew casually. He had been quite ill the last year or two, I knew, and had been hospitalized several times. He said he was no longer allowed to work at all because of his heart condition and was going crazy doing nothing but sitting in the house and driving his wife crazy. Everything made him terribly nervous now. And how was my summer?

I told him about my eyes and that my car had to go. Could he buy it for his college-age daughter? I didn't know yet, I said; probably one of my family would get it. He then quickly asked if he could drive me, anywhere, anytime. It would give him something to do, something to look forward to. Hurray! but could and should I accept it? "I'll make a bargain with you. You drive me and as we go we can talk about anything that bothers or annoys you, and that way you can get things off your chest." (Did he know I was a social worker?) It was settled. From then on, to the doctors, dentists, hairdresser, sometimes the library, and gradually we became each other's boyfriend and girlfriend in spite of almost thirty years' difference. One of the lovely things about this gentle man was his quick and cheerful "No problem!" whenever I called. Why can't more people say brightly, "No problem" instead of pondering possibilities?

A neighbor on the other side, whose doctor husband went very early to his hospital and so used their carport, kept her car in her space next to mine. From my kitchen window I used to watch her scrape snow or rime or ice off her automobile before starting off for work. I sympathized. I also knew she did her weekly food shopping Saturday mornings. I called her and suggested that since I was selling my car she might like to use my carport on a permanent basis, and maybe in exchange she would take me with her on her Saturday shopping. Again the perfect solution. And we've developed a nice friendship.

But the day came when my lovely three-year-old car, now sold to my midwestern son, backed out, turned, and went. . . . Forever. I stood and watched with my hand on my doorknob in incredible emptiness. For with that car departed its mint and dentless condition, its mere 11,000 miles, my perfectly adjusted driver's seat, Alec's inherited four-digit number plate, my "Antique Beaver" C.B. radio. All my love for that one inanimate object which represented independence and maneuverability and freedom to go—gone! After sixty-four years never to put my foot to the starter or brake again, never lay my hands on a steering wheel, never to float off whither I would . . . Oh, what the hell!

My friends heard my unspoken words. There were many offers to take me places, and I learned for the first time how to sit relaxed while others drove, to relax and look around. Women are apt to be erratic and jerky drivers, each sure of herself in her familiarity with her own ways, but I found the greatest variation as a passenger. One always pulling a little to the right, then jerking back, one going too fast, one coming to stops suddenly and braking, one taking hands off the wheel when she talked. I learned and I learned to sit patiently while others did their errands. I also found I could ask for help now quite easily and cleanly with none of the guilt I used to feel when it was my back that was limiting me.

With the determination that I would "not go gentle into the good night," as Dylan Thomas said, "Blind eyes should blaze like meteors and be gay," I tackled the house. Grocery cabinets—one item deep, everything easily recognizable, no fishing in the back; extra shelves put on the rears of closet doors to hold extra supplies; pointed strips of luminous red tape stuck on every last indicator, from thermostat to radios to scales to thermometers both in and out; an inch-wide red strip painted on the edge of the front steps and an iron rail installed there. All herbs labeled in big print on a hanging wall shelf, most pots, pans, and covers in sight, as artistically placed as possible; knives slapped against a very strong magnet, no longer in slots. The list was endless.

Before long I acquired, for three hours a week, an incredibly mature and efficient secretary to open and pay bills, do accounts, and read letters in small print. I invested in a large-type typewriter, and found my hand and finger exercises were paying off beautifully. My telephone list was redone in big black lettering.

In the summer friends had given me as a birthday present the large-print *New York Times* weekly edition; now I took the *Reader's Digest;* then, as my inquiries went farther, I discovered an entire network to which nobody seemed to have a single directory or even a key. Through my oculist's signed statement of my limitations, through sending confirmation to the state, through the state via somebody in Cambridge, then through the federal government, came free, free! a brand, brand new four-track cassette player and an 8 RPM record player—the only things I've ever had free from the government since my original birth certificate eighty years ago. But I found great difficulty getting books of any substance. Libraries of course carry large-print books, which I could still read under very bright light, but they were "soft" reading, which fitted in nicely with the prevailing idea of the elderly or the eye-handicapped as universally dumb or reluctant to be stimulated. Certainly in the book catalogues that eventually began coming, every single book, classic or not, was rated for its content—"some violence" or "some sex," or "explicit sex." But somewhere, somewhere, when I can trace it down, must be a place of real and nourishing works. I have a great and overwhelming desire to begin my education in those areas I've missed before.

But the most fun of all that fall, after my agent had the two perfect copies of my book in hand and had passed them on to a publisher, was the emptying my mind by emptying the house. I'd done it other times before, but there's always more to go, particularly when you project your mind into sternly reduced activity. Every drawer, cupboard, shelf, closet, storage place, and the huge cellar were gone over with a fine-tooth comb for any duplicates or unneeded articles, and though I loved my leather-bound books as part of the warmth and decor of my house, there were many others about the family, photograph books, unusual editions. I would not ever read them again.

Reduce! Reduce! And the bubble of an idea was there, for let's have fun while we're at it.

I could remember so well the total body excitement in those rare childhood chances at a "grab bag" at a lawn fete or small fair.

The big closed bag, or tub with a slit in the paper cover, and you went up timidly, with your ten cents held tight (how sticky and greasy a coin felt when thus held too long) and you presented it and the moment came and you could thrust in your arm and pull out the first thing you touched—a little parcel in white paper and tied with ribbon or string. The suspense! Would it be some boy's top or something worth only one cent? Would it be a treasure? No, my memory is that it was the excitement, the chance, the bet, the unknown that was the thrill. Will I? Won't I? Yes? No? (Why didn't I become a gambler?)

Now with all these things I was clearing out, a childlike glee overcame me. I would make a tremendous grab bag for the thirteen young (ages twenty to thirty) adults at my Christmas party to come. We never really grow up, do we? At least we shouldn't. I went to work. The June before, at a sidewalk sale, I had spotted a huge roll of wallpaper. It was a gold and silver modernistic design, incredibly awful for walls but perfect for Christmas presents. I bought it for seventy-nine cents. Now, this late November, I discovered in my box of Christmas stuff in the cellar, unused for three years, two huge rolls of good ribbon, one gold color, the other white and silver.

It was so simple to do up Christmas presents when there is one card table, one roll of paper, one of ribbon, one of Scotch tape and a pair of scissors. No decisions, no matching up, no labels, no pen. I became enchanted and the work went incredibly fast, even though I did it at leisure. Everything under a foot in size I did up in boxes, large and small, saved for years and overloading a corner of the cellar. In my excitement I went around discovering more and more things, for grab bags can hold a new pad of paper as well as gold watches, and watches were no use to me now without a large dial. And at the end of wrapping these smaller presents, I had a stack in the guest room closet of over one hundred and fifty.

What about the large things? The electric floor polisher? The complete set of china? The set of pots and pans? The electric weather vane? The extra plumber's helper? The copper flower trays? My collection of fossils? Some lovely big baskets? Two party tablecloths? On and on. With my secretary's help they were laid out in rows on the cellar floor, each in a carton or tote bag, each gum-taped shut, unwrapped but out of sight, all marked with large black numbers. There on the cellar floor they lay, thirty-nine of them. And upstairs were the thirty-nine numbered cards that would be drawn by chance.

This Christmas was very, very important in some way. Five years before, no Christmas, Alec had just died. Four years before, no time for Christmas, I had just moved. Three years ago, though presents were there, my back was in spasm and my soul and mind were in disarray. Two years before I was so crumpled and semi-invalided that Christmas was empty; last year I had been in the Pain Unit except for a few hours Christmas noon. But *this* year would be *Christmas!*

It was.

We were twenty-one in all. Granddaughters made four different quiches, several salads, helped me set up the table for self-service. Several days before on the big windowsill and on a table I had lovingly placed the hundred-fifty-plus golden presents, with string after string of miniature lights making them like little Christmas trees. And for several days I kept going in to look and admire, and I kept the lights on for myself at night.

All arrived including little Alana, sixteen months old, the only great-grandchild, in a bright red velvet dress that had belonged to her mother's biggest doll when she was a child, and Alana had thrown up just before she reached the house after her hour's drive, thrown up all over her snowsuit and her mother's coat and feet. But these were cleaned up. And the whole evening that little girl trotted happily between and among the feet of the elders, utterly relaxed in a strange place and with strangers, and only now and then glancing at her parents' faces.

The eggnog made by special recipe of my son-in-law started us off. There was beer in plenty as well as hard liquor. The fire blazed, and the room was mostly lit by candles and Christmas lights. The cousins all caught up, we drank, we ate, and anticipation rose and rose. All! Those! Presents! We, the elderly and middle-aged relations, were the observers.

Finally came the announcements and I sat like the queen I was. My son-in-law announced the engagement of his oldest daughter. Cheers and toasts. It was the first Christmas of a great-grandchild in the family. Cheers and drinks. I made a speech.

I said the only magazine in our house when I was a child, aside from *St. Nicholas* and the *Youth's Companion,* was the *Atlantic Monthly*. And now the Atlantic Monthly Press had taken my book with a slight condition on the revision (loud cheers, more drinks), and then I announced a Christmas present, to all, that the previous October, when the book was worth nothing, I had given the manuscript to my Irrevocable Trust. And would they all please drink to the success of the book so the trust would earn enough from it to pay me for my outlay in expenses so far? Cheers. They drank.

And as candles glowed, Christmas lights twinkled, little velveted Alana ran among the feet and against knees, dragging her new noisy quack-quack duck on wheels, and then I announced, "Grab bag. You're all children. You take what you get. Exchange, swap if you don't like anything, bid, give away, throw away, but one rule. Everything, but everything, whether you want it or not, goes out of this house tonight *with* containers and papers."

The chosen Santa and helper went around the great circle with the presents now in a huge basket. Hilarity arose, there was confusion, bidding began, voices raised, absorption was utter and complete (the older adults got their presents from a special pile). And when it came to giving out the cards with their large numbers, they were shuffled, everybody came up and pulled out three, and we all streamed down the cellar stairs. It was mad, ridiculous, noisy, and too confusing to possibly follow the complicated exchanges and laughter that went on.

At some point after that I went to my room, closed the door, and flopped into bed, leaving everyone going strong, even the tireless, tearless little red Alana.

But about four o'clock in the morning I woke and slipped out to check. The lights were off. Guest room door closed, the thermostat turned down, the door locked, an enormous grandson asleep on the mattress he had lugged up from the cellar to the middle of the living room floor, and as I lit up the room not a speck of anything was in sight. Floor vacuumed, Christmas lights all carefully coiled and fastened with an elastic, ornaments, pillows in place. The kitchen? Immaculate, the dishwasher still faintly warm from its cycle. I went down cellar, betting that there would be some omission. There wasn't. Swept clean, not a box, not a bit of excelsior. Immaculate. Oh you great and wonderful young ones—I love you!

And I went back to sleep, for *now* I had at last had my Christmas! A child's perfect Christmas! The one I had always wanted and never had in my eighty years.

A letdown in the after-silence of Christmas in my now empty house? Yes, but only in terms of sliding into a calm contemplation of what there was now. What had I, if worse came to worst? I could hear Milton speak: "Why should I not submit with complacency to the loss of my sight, which seems only to withdraw from the body without to increase the sight of the mind within?" Right. But in the calm of my days, I took note also of the wise body's quiet message, defining for me, over and over, the wide boundaries of human existence. I like to think of the tides of breath, of my circadian rhythms, even though my awareness is chiefly confined to jet flight, that I have a bird's sense of direction even though it be vestigial, that moving clockwise or counterclockwise has its own subtle difference, that I respond deeply to the passing of the seasons, that I am always aware of the powers of the sun and pull of the moon (why don't calendars nowadays remind us of its changes?) and that I am as a plumb bob to the ground.

If I don't insist on seeing in my old way, my confused vision need see not a shape per se, but instead the new planes and lines and shadows and luminousness that emerge. The same occurs outside with landscapes.

There are delicious personal memories waiting, and those from the collective unconscious that flutter up unbidden. There is the self-study of self and its drives: and of selflessness and its stillnesses. Sometimes the right brain moves to create with potent urgency and cogent force. More and more inner paths open toward awareness. All these things I thought and readied myself for.

And then, one day, in my mailbox, *it* came, the ultimate gift. I had located its existence at last, no thanks to the state agencies for the blind, which hold the prevailing attitude of superiority toward the elderly of "poor sweet dumb things." *It* came and I had it! That fat, fat catalogue from "Recording for the Blind!" And bless forever those philanthropic souls who make possible the more than fifty thousand cassettes of classic or scholarly works. All free for the borrowing, with four thousand more books added yearly, and free recording of any special volume one desires. Even free mailing. Manna for a fasting mind! Simply insert the tape and press the appropriate button! Looking at that catalogue, I might have been looking at the world's first sunrise.

And now death and I can go romping along, keeping pace together, for no matter how low I am laid, I can lie and listen and vibrate to those voices, all those voices in all those tongues speaking to and of and in creation.

As my mind is open, so too is the door of my house, and my heart is full of warmth toward those I love.

The time may come for me, too, when the bladder, bowels, heart, blood pressure, veins, bones, and digestion all misbehave, misact, miscue: any or all of them. Singly, or all at once. Would I have to "cruelize" myself then? If this book were in print at that time I would loan it to myself and say, "Can't you remember?"

No longer am I on a quest for the quiet West, or for a moment of enlightenment, or for nirvana or satori. No longer do I think to wear the vestal calm of a truly wise woman, or feel I bear the patient watchfulness of the Mother of all the World who carries pain in her heart.

I prefer my weal and woe, and my own physical pain, which still claims me but to which I can usually sit soft and light, and I prefer my glorious wild inner freedom and sometimes great abandoned physical gestures. I prefer to flow on a river of curiosity and insight and creativity and compassion as and when they sweep me on, a river where I am always in that state of becoming which carries its own immediate pain.

I have kept faith with my unbelief, and though there have been fear and no signposts to follow, out of this very unbelief has come such trust in the sight of the mind within that perhaps I will one day be vouchsafed a final vision of myself in the universe, the universe in me.

Each morning now, usually about dawn, tightening the belt of my dressing gown as I go, I move from my bed space to my shining little kitchen space, there to turn on the heat under the teakettle. Today the smell of my house is warm to me, the birds are fluttering around the feeder, and the refrigerator purrs. And in that little distance and in that repetition I know all the happiness I need to know, for I can now live immediacy without rattling the dice of the past or rolling out those of the future. My bondage to the wheel of life and death is light.

The snow fell heavily as I slept, and under the rising sun it was softening and dropping from the trees. I remembered back, back to my envy of Alec's ability to fall off trees in spirit. Suddenly he and I fused into one another again. I, in life, fused with Alec in death.

Oh, Alec! Alec!